FAITH WITH REASON

Why Christianity Is True

Joseph R. Farinaccio

BookSpecs Publishing
Pennsville, New Jersey

Published by BookSpecs Publishing
16 Sunset Ave.
Pennsville, NJ 08070
www.FaithWithReason.com

**Publisher's Cataloging-in-Publication Data
(Provided by Quality Books, Inc.)**

Farinaccio, Joseph R.
    Faith with reason : why Christianity is true / Joseph
    R. Farinaccio. -- 1st ed.
    p. cm.
    LCCN 2002092455
    ISBN 978-0-9903276-8-4

    1. Apologetics. 2. Christianity and other religions.
    3. Christianity and culture. 4. Philosophy and religion. I. Title.

BT1102.F37 2002   239
                              QBI33-569

This book is dedicated
to my mother,
Anne Dorothy Farinaccio,
and my wife,
Joni Lynn Farinaccio,
- constant encouragers.

Acknowledgements

There are individuals whose contributions, both large and small, help turn someone's idea into a reality. This book is no exception. Each of them contributed something special, not the least of which was their time. My parents, Joseph and Anne Farinaccio, are treasured gifts from God. Christian Education director Rev. David Hutchinson offered a theological critique. English instructor Vincent Farinaccio provided editorial skills. Fellow church member Linda Smookler made numerous manuscript corrections and offered insightful suggestions. Longtime friend George Perez created the book cover. My brother Paul Farinaccio furnished a logo. Pastor and theologian Charles Betters offered his endorsement. And my family - Joni, Matthew and Nicole all patiently allowed me to spend many hours in front of the computer. I can never say "Thank You" enough to all of you.

Joseph Farinaccio
Vineland, New Jersey
June 2002

CONTENTS

Introduction

This is a book about worldviews. Everybody has one, but most individuals never really pay much attention to their own personal philosophy of life. This is a tragedy because there is no state of awareness so fundamental to living life. Since there are many worldviews out there this book was written to help individuals understand why biblical Christianity is so important, not only in our understanding of God, but ourselves and the world around us as well.

Every subject we think about is filtered through our worldview. The picture of reality we hold in our minds is what we use at the most basic level to answer every question in life. This is especially true of big questions, like those pertaining to man's origin, ethics, life's meaning and ultimate destiny. This makes faith central to every aspect of our lives and being. The bigger question, of course, is whether or not the picture of reality we have is actually true.

Several 20th century Christian philosophers were very influential in bringing attention to the subject of worldviews. Cornelius Van Til, Greg Bahnsen, and Francis Schaeffer are considerable influences upon the thinking of many Christians, including myself. Most of what is contained in these pages is simply a re-statement of fundamental truths they addressed. Yet there were several reasons why I wanted to offer a collection of thoughts based upon their philosophical work.

First, this book attempts to quickly get to the heart of the matter. Presuppositions are the heart of everyone's view of reality. I wanted to offer people, especially young adults, a concise summary of some very important concepts. A few hours spent reading the material here will sharpen the thinking of believers and challenge those who think that "science" or "reason" actually serves as the foundation for true knowledge.

Next, I wanted to focus on some of the fundamental topics that repeatedly come up in conversations between Christians and non-Christians. For this reason each chapter is really an individual essay that focuses on a particular subject.

Finally, I wanted to present the philosophy of Christianity in relatively simple language and style. This book is geared for a popular audience. Most people are not professional philosophers and do not care to be. But almost any mature person can and should recognize that they are constantly being confronted with truth-claims from various worldviews. Everyone has a faith and the world needs to know what sets apart the Bible's truth-claims from others.

Many people only pretend to seek truth in order to justify their preconceived notions of reality. Others are genuinely searching for what is often called *ultimate* truth. I wanted to share with such individuals that it is possible to know that God does not just offer real answers to our questions. He's the one who created us to ask meaningful questions in the first place.

1

Can All Views Be True?

Is it possible for Christians to claim that their belief system is true? Is the very claim itself an example of religious intolerance? Most public discussion of religion in contemporary culture is overshadowed by the notion that anyone may hold religious views as long as they do not say others are inferior.

All belief systems make truth-claims. Truth-claims by their very nature imply that contrary assertions are false. It is impossible for two genuinely opposite truth-claims to be simultaneously true. Although the law of contradiction may not be popular when applied to religious beliefs, it is still undeniable "that two antithetical propositions cannot both be true at the same time and in the same sense. X cannot be non-X. A thing cannot be and not be simultaneously. And nothing that is true can be self-contradictory or inconsistent with any other truth. All logic depends on this simple principle. Rational thought and meaningful discourse demand it."[1]

This runs counter to the relativistic thinking that is so popular with many in our culture today. Large numbers of people tend to think that all belief systems, especially "religious" ones, must be viewed as equal.

> In the worldview of religious diversity, all religions are equal *even if they're contradictory*. No one religion is any more true than any other religion. While this makes for happy harmony on paper, in the real world it just doesn't work. Try asserting diversity in the following areas:

- "It just doesn't matter what you believe about *mathematics,* as long as you're sincere in your beliefs."

- "It doesn't matter what you believe about *electromagnetism,* as long as you're sincere in your beliefs."

- "It doesn't matter what you believe about *Nazism,* as long as you're sincere in your beliefs."

- "It doesn't matter what you believe about *slavery,* as long as you're sincere in your beliefs."

Few people would tolerate such nonsense, but many are very comfortable with the notion that all religions are valid even when they are contradictory.[2]

All beliefs are not equal. The theory of Evolution and biblical Creationism may be studied as two separate views about origins, but both of them cannot be true. It is irrational to declare the equality of all truth-claims, especially those made by rival religions.

The history of religion is filled with countless movements involving believers who either desired to correct older views or establish new ones. Tension between differing religious ideas has existed all throughout human history. But the need to exercise true tolerance towards others' beliefs does not mean that one has to champion the irrational idea that all views are equally true. Christianity, like *all* belief systems, is exclusive in the sense that it asserts its claims are true.

There is nothing wrong with believing that some things are true and others false. "Although many accuse absolutists of intolerance, these accusers most likely have an unclear and distorted notion of what tolerance really is. They are often unaware that the concept of tolerance implies a close relationship to truth. Contrary to popular definitions, true tolerance means 'putting up with error' - not 'being accepting of all views'...It is because real differences exist between people that tolerance becomes necessary and virtuous."[3] Christianity's adherents include both converted Jews and Gentiles. The Christian faith crosses racial, ethnic, social, lingual, and national boundaries. It includes all people groups, from every nation, tribe, kindred, and tongue. (Rev 7:9) Its *membership* is inclusive and diverse, but its *belief system* is exclusive and dogmatic.

Biblical Christianity rejects the falsehood that all beliefs are equal. As a belief system it claims to present truth about God, man, and the world. While the Bible directs Christians to be sensitive towards others' feelings it nonetheless admonishes those same believers to "Go into all the world and preach the good news to all creation. Whoever believes and is baptized will be saved, but whoever does not believe will be condemned." (Mark 16:15-16)

To reject this Christian view, or any other worldview, means that one prefers *another view* of reality. Worldviews are ultimate. They govern our entire outlook on life. We make judgements about everything, especially other views, with our current worldview. Those who challenge the integrity of the Bible as God's Word do so because they have adopted another worldview. No one may legitimately say, "I don't *know* what view is right, but I *know* that you're wrong." The reason why anyone thinks another view is wrong is because they believe their view (whatever it may be) is correct.

It is not possible, of course, for any human being to provide an *exhaustive* explanation of the nature of reality. But the fact that we cannot know everything about reality should not be used as an excuse to believe anything we want to. It is only rational to assume that the metaphysical beliefs posited by any given belief system should not conflict with each another. And those same beliefs should also collectively reveal a metaphysical framework that can genuinely account for reality, including man's origin and place within it.

No worldview provides comprehensive answers. It is impossible to have every single one of our questions exhaustively answered. Yet skeptics often single out Christianity for failing to answer every conceivable question they may have about God or the Bible. Why demand something from Christianity without requiring the same from their worldview? Yet such double standards are common among Christianity's critics. Comprehensive answers are not possible for creatures with finite minds. There are many things that will remain a mystery to us in this life. (1Cor 13:12) But lack of comprehensive information does not mean one cannot have confidence in the Bible's truth-claims.

The main question each of us need to ask ourselves is this, "Why do I think my current belief system is true?" Rejecting one view in favor of another should be accompanied by more than just a superficial nod at the big questions of life, and intellectual honesty demands more than casually ignoring the truth-claims of orthodox Christianity without really investigating them.

All of us to some degree harbor certain biases for believing what we do. Christians certainly want the Bible to be authentic in its revelation of God, but that is not a valid reason for believing its truth-claims. Christian believers, however, are not the only ones with biases. There are those, for example, who self-consciously construct their worldview so that it does not include God:

> In speaking of the fear of religion, I don't mean to refer to the entirely reasonable hostility toward certain established religions...in virtue of their objectionable moral doctrines, social policies, and political influence. Nor am I referring to the association of many religious beliefs with superstition and the acceptance of evident empirical

falsehoods. I am talking about something much deeper – namely, the fear of religion itself.... I want atheism to be true and am made uneasy by the fact that some of the most intelligent and well-informed people I know are religious believers. It isn't just that I don't believe in God and naturally, hope there is no God! I don't want there to be a God; I don't want the universe to be like that.[4]

This professing atheist recognized that worldviews have implications. Beliefs shape the way we look at the world and determine how we will interpret the particular facts of the world all around us. This is no small issue. "To commit one's life, habits, thoughts, goals, priorities – everything – to a certain world-view with no questions asked is, from the antagonist's point of view, to build one's life upon a very questionable foundation."[5] This makes it all the more necessary to seriously consider what is implied by ultimate truth-claims. All of the world's religions and philosophies hold certain views regarding "God, man, and the Cosmos."[6] The world contains many differing conceptions of reality.[7]

It is the evangelical Christian's contention that "anti-Christianity in all its forms is arbitrary. We see it to be held together by will power, energy of assertion, and the turning of a blind eye to awkward facts rather than by force of evidence or cogency of argument."[8] These are serious charges. But the apologists for any belief system must attempt to show why their view is truer than other ones. This is a part of the journey of discovering faith with reason.

2

Presuppositions and Worldviews

Each of us is an individual creature in a vast universe. We are finite beings with limits to our knowledge. We cannot and do not know everything there is to know. This means that in order to reason about anything at all we must first *assume* certain things about reality.

At the heart of every philosophy of life are certain basic assumptions about what is real and true. Everyone has these assumptions or presuppositions about what they perceive reality to be. Day to day thinking involves the use of premises from which we draw conclusions. But these premises are themselves based upon certain *assumptions* about reality. When baking a loaf of leavened bread, for example, experienced bakers know that proper ingredients in right proportions, along with a consistent yeast temperature, are all required. But their premises are based on a very general assumption that the bread-making process requires the same ingredients and procedures today as in the past. It is assumed that the *present* will be like the *past*. Bakers, in this case, are presupposing that *nature is uniform*.

The assumption that nature is uniform is a primary assumption we use every day. In fact, it is a prerequisite for scientific methodology. But this assumption is not *proven* by science. Scientists *assume* that uniformity in nature is true so that experiments can be performed. The fact that scientists observe uniformity within their limited experiences does not prove its *universality* nor does it guarantee that uniformity will still hold true *tomorrow*. Science operates upon a belief in the uniformity of nature even though it does not account for it. Presuppositions of science, logic or morality are not natural objects of the universe.

They are merely held by individuals to be true. They are presupposed. They are assumed – *by faith*.

In order to reason about any subject each of us must presuppose the existence of certain *pre-conditions* in order to form the premises from which we'll draw our conclusions. Since presuppositions lie at the heart of our beliefs about reality they should be identified. Yet how many of us ever stop to think about what they are? Have we ever considered the role they play in ultimately shaping our worldview or their influence upon how we think and reason?

The following presuppositions are assumed in various belief systems:

• A personal God has revealed Himself to man as recorded in the Bible (Christianity)

• There is no personal deity (Atheism)

• Universal economic laws are the driving force behind history (Marxism)

• Rational thought is the best way to arrive at ultimate truth (Rationalism)

• The universe is essentially made up of matter and energy (Materialism)

• The material world is not real, it's only an illusion (Hinduism)

• Freedom is a human property each of us possesses that must be exercised through individual choices for which each person alone is responsible (Existentialism)

Presuppositions are at the heart of worldviews. What exactly is a worldview? The English word for *worldview* comes from "the German *weltanschaaung*. It literally means a life perspective or way of seeing. It is simply the way we look at the world. You have a worldview. I have a worldview. Everyone does. It is our perspective. It is our frame of reference. It is the means by which we interpret the situations and circumstances around us. It is what enables us to integrate all the different aspects of our faith, and life, and experience... A worldview is simply a way of viewing the world."[9] Our worldview is our life view wherein we try to integrate the sum and substance of life together in a way that makes sense to us. It represents our personal metaphysical outlook on life.

Our most basic assumptions or presuppositions about reality collectively form the foundation of our worldview. Presuppositions are interconnected. They work together to form a web of basic beliefs. These presuppositions shape our worldview grid. This becomes the screen through which we interpret our whole universe.

> The beliefs which people hold are always connected to *other* beliefs by relations pertaining to linguistic meaning, logical order, evidential dependence, causal explanation, indexical and self-conceptions, etc. To assert "I see a ladybug on the rose" is to affirm and assume a *number* of things simultaneously-some rather obvious (e.g., about the usage of English words, one's personal identity, a perceptual event, categories of bugs and flowers, physical relations), others more subtle (e.g., about one's linguistic, entomological, and botanical competence, the normalcy of one's eyes and brain-stem, theories of light refraction, shared grammar and semantics, the reality of the external world, laws of logic, etc.).[10]

Since presuppositions, such as the uniformity of nature, are simply taken for granted our worldview is ultimately a faith-view.

Every view of life, expressly religious or supposedly non-religious, is a belief system that begins with assumptions held by faith. Even worldviews that are not officially based upon a canon of scripture, a declared creed, or some other formal religious system are filled with faith nonetheless.

The essence of every worldview is rooted in its transcendent, metaphysical, governing assumptions about the nature of reality. It is never really a question of which of us exercises faith and which one doesn't. Faith is something within all of us. "All men presuppose, whatever the name they use for it, a synoptic view of reality as a whole. We continue to call it metaphysics."[11]

Many people seek to construct their own worldview themselves. They try to come up with answers about ultimate reality on their own when they do this. They are essentially saying, "I think that reality consists of such and such…etc." But those who adhere to a biblical worldview do not rely upon their own arbitrary assumptions as a tool to construct their own explanations for what exists. They begin by assuming what the Bible reveals about reality is true.

Christians and non-Christians begin thinking about every subject from their own worldview perspective. They have different worldviews. Worldviews play a central role in discussions about God, man and the cosmos. They touch the very core of what we believe about reality. It should not be surprising then that worldview clashes occur. Every one of us will disagree with worldviews that are different from our own.

Christians regard the Bible as ultimate authority within their worldview because it is assumed to be the true Word of God. Those who wish to adhere to a biblical worldview consciously attempt to think about every area of life from a biblical perspective. Every biblical truth is taken as a Christian presupposition that will be held in faith as part of their whole biblical outlook on life. Bible-believing Christians assume that

God has spoken with authority and also presuppose, in accordance with scripture, that what God has revealed in the Bible is true.

The bottom line is that everyone reasons through a view of reality that is rooted in faith-based assumptions about the reality they perceive to be true. Everyone has a faith-based worldview which means there are no neutral areas of life. Every aspect of being and activity is interpreted through our worldview grid.

3
Faith and Reason

Both secularism[12] and relativism[13] heavily influence Western society. Secularism is currently applied in government, academia, and public education. Its familiar mantra is "separation of church and state." While its goal supposedly is to promote religious "neutrality" in state funded institutions it is clearly anti-religious. The so-called "separation" principal is almost always used to keep religious beliefs from influencing any arena that receives "public" monies. Religion is only encouraged to take place within a personal-private sphere. The result is that many public institutions limit religious activity in an effort to keep it out of the public square.

Why is Secularism so opposed to religion? Many secularists argue that all types of religious dogmatism (especially the kind contained in creeds and professions of faith) should be restricted in the interest of keeping people's personal religious beliefs from negatively affecting others who have different beliefs. This means public institutions must attempt to be religiously neutral. The perception that faith-beliefs should no longer be permitted to influence public institutions or policy in the interest of fairness to everyone is now widely regarded as a prerequisite for civil liberty.

Behind this secularist view of religion often lies a conviction that faith-views are really beyond empirical verification or rational proof. Secular intellectuals frequently treat contemporary religious belief as little more than superstition. Many advocates of secularism contend that it was not God who created man but rather man who has created the idea of God. In their view civilization can advance only as it moves beyond such ancient religious "myths" in favor of enlightened reason and modern science. True knowledge, they contend, is found through rational or empirical means.

Western popular culture promotes relativism. Relativism's major premise is that no absolute truth exists except that there is no absolute truth. The attempt to discard a belief in absolute truth then leads people to affirm that everyone is entitled to hold certain personal beliefs no one else has the right to question or judge. Supposedly religious beliefs cannot be tested for truth and therefore everyone's beliefs must be regarded as equal. Everyone is entitled to religious beliefs free from rational scrutiny and may choose whatever faith-views they want to.

Both secularism and relativism have come about largely as a result of a misunderstanding of the faith-reason relationship. Faith and reason are usually defined in such a way as to mean that religious ideas have no connection with logic. The *Internet Encyclopedia of Philosophy* explains the relationship between faith and reason in the following way:

> Reason generally is understood as the principles for a methodological inquiry... Some kind of algorithmic *demonstrability* is ordinarily presupposed. Once demonstrated, a proposition or claim is ordinarily understood to be justified as true or authoritative. Faith, on the other hand, involves a stance toward some claim that is not...demonstrable by reason. Thus faith is a kind of attitude of trust or assent.[14]

The preceding definition portrays faith as a subjective attitude towards some belief one wishes to affirm. Some secular skeptics have gone even further and defined faith-beliefs as superstitious notions that thrive only in the absence of reason or science. They see faith in terms of something one believes in that is either lacking in or entirely contrary to reason. These views of faith and reason are mistaken because all reason is ultimately based upon certain *presuppositions* within our worldview. Faith and reason are firmly connected. Every belief system is a *faith* system because its presuppositions are ultimately faith commitments. Secular beliefs have their own particular set of faith based presuppositions. *Reason is not separated from faith; reason is based upon faith.*

If all reasoning is based upon certain basic *assumptions* about reality then faith and reason are always linked together. This is exactly the opposite of how most people see the relationship between them. They do not understand that faith actually *precedes* reason. Reason is not opposed to faith in itself. Faith is not something we "leap"[15] to after leaving reason behind. Faith is not a leap but rather a foundation.

Faith is present prior to our thinking about any subject. We all reason from the perspective of an established worldview. We begin with faith presuppositions and then use them to reason. Our faith assumptions are the foundation for all our reasoning. There is not one subject area where conclusions do not involve primary assumptions held by faith. The fact that we all view the world according to some set of assumptions about reality means that we all have a faith-view. Presuppositions are at the heart of every worldview regardless of whether that worldview is religious or secular.

Trying to say that logic does not apply to religious beliefs is also self-contradictory. To *reason* about faith in such a way as to argue that reason is not applied in matters of faith is disingenuous. All thoughts, including religious ones, rest upon certain presuppositions. These assumptions about reality should not only be identified, they should also be justified. Questioning our underlying assumptions about reality to see if they can account for the reality of the world in which we live is not unreasonable.

The U.S. Supreme Court has even recognized the faith element that lies at the heart of all belief systems, whether secular or religious. In 1961 the High Court wrote, "Among *religions* in this country which do not teach what would generally be considered a belief in the existence of God are Buddhism, Taoism, Ethical Culture, *Secular Humanism* and others."[16] A few years later, in United States v. Seeger, the Court reassessed its approach to religious terminology by saying it would now "construe the words 'Supreme Being' to include the cosmos."[17] "Thus, according to the justices in *Seeger*, *religion* includes atheism and agnosticism."[18] For the Supreme Court to recognize the faith-based nature of all worldviews while simultaneously affirming the idea that public institutions must somehow remain free from "religious" influences is clearly a contradiction.

Presuppositions lie at the very foundation of reason. Reasoning necessarily presupposes certain laws of logic that govern right from wrong thinking. Such laws would have to be immaterial, universally binding, and unchanging. Some philosophers have tried to argue that there really are no "laws" of logic per se. Instead, they suggest logic is merely a descriptive term for a set of rules established by either language or social constructs. But this explanation hardly provides a foundation for what we call logic. For "without logical laws even simple everyday conversation would be impossible...even at the level of word usage, we *already* presuppose basic logical distinctions. That is, logic is necessary for language even to get off the ground."[19]

The confusion over faith's proper relationship to reason has led many people to think that religious beliefs should not be scrutinized. Attempting to judge another's faith-beliefs, participate in religious debate, or engage in any type of evangelistic activity now often conveys a perception of bigotry or intolerance. While it certainly may be legitimate to criticize the manner in which some of these activities take place there should never be a question as to whether or not beliefs and ideas (especially religious ones) may be truth-tested or debated.

When it comes to questions of personal faith-beliefs we need to understand that while we may enjoy the political freedom to hold irrational views we do not have an intellectual right to believe whatever we want. An analogy would be the belief in Santa Claus. Many of us once thought Santa Claus was real. It is acceptable for children to believe in Santa Claus. But if we continued to believe in Santa Claus as teenagers our parents would have been understandably concerned. As we grow older we are expected to correspond our beliefs with rational thinking. Yet when it comes to certain religious or secular beliefs this rule is often abandoned.

Many people tend to view their faith-beliefs as "sacred cows" that cannot be touched. The theory of Evolution is a prime example. Evolutionists have figured out that the best way to insulate this doctrine from scrutiny is to prevent a debate from ever beginning in the first place. Intellectual criticisms of evolution's dogmas are vehemently resisted on the grounds that "religious" views must not mix with "science." Reasoned challenges to evolution are simply dismissed as Creationism (religious attacks) in disguise.

Secular and religious views both have their own unique faith-beliefs. Darwinism believes that uncreated, random matter and energy interacted within an undirected and unsupervised process to create what now exists in the universe, including man. Materialistic atheism begins with the assumption that there is no God because only matter and energy can be known to exist. Orthodox Hinduism conceives that this physical world does not really exist because physical matter is only an illusion.

Everyone has a particular view of reality they believe is true. Belief systems posit truth-claims that are implied to be *objective* in nature because they offer an explanation for reality. Life is built upon the perception that objective truth exists with regard to this reality. Truth then cannot be dependent upon personal preferences. Relativism's ultimate assumption that absolute truth does not exist is false because it is self-contradictory. Relativism asserts that there is no such thing as absolute truth even as it posits this belief to be absolutely true. For relativists to be consistent with their own position they would have to admit that the supposed truth of relativism itself is relative, which completely undermines it.

Since all worldviews contain beliefs that their adherents consider to be true, the important question then becomes, "How is it possible to know if these beliefs are true or not?" Christians maintain that one can have knowledge that the things written in the Bible are true. "The conflict between believers and unbelievers is ultimately over the differing worldviews – networks of pre-suppositions in terms of which experience is interpreted and reasoning is guided."[20]

Faith-beliefs are at the heart of every worldview. Theistic and non-theistic worldviews alike compete for both attention and supremacy in the mind of every human being. The ideas contained in them produce consequences for both individuals and cultures. Because of this a proper understanding of how faith and reason interact is one of the most important concepts anyone can ever comprehend.

4

Christian Presuppositions

I believe in God, the Father, the Almighty, Maker of heaven and earth, and in Jesus Christ, His only begotten Son, our Lord, Who was conceived by the Holy Spirit, born of the Virgin Mary, Suffered under Pontius Pilate, was crucified, dead, and buried; He descended into hades; the third day He arose again from the dead; He ascended into heaven and sits on the right hand of God the Father Almighty; from there He shall come to judge the living and the dead. I believe in the Holy Spirit, the holy catholic church, the communion of saints, the forgiveness of sins, the resurrection of the body, and the life everlasting. AMEN.

-The Apostle's Creed

The historic creeds of Christendom, especially the Apostle's Creed, have long been used to express certain fundamental doctrines within the Christian faith. In one sense, any meaningful exposition of scripture is a type of creed. Creeds are seen "in the biblical record of apostolic Christianity itself... perhaps the most familiar of these rudimentary creeds is the recurrent one embedded in such texts as Acts 10:36; Romans 10:9; 1 Corinthians 12:3; and Philippians 2:11 - Jesus is Lord."[21] Statements of belief that resemble formal creeds are also seen in 1Corinthians 15:4 and 1Timothy 3:16.

The creeds are examples of carefully constructed statements of faith meant to "define the content of belief."[22] C*reed* comes from the Latin *credo*, meaning, "I believe." "If anyone believes anything

24

he has a creed. And since it is not possible for a person to live his life without believing something, then everyone has a creed."[23]

At present, many of the largest ecclesiastical organizations once doctrinally conformed to the historic creedal affirmations no longer firmly hold to them. The question is why? Are today's liberal theologians somehow wiser than the ancient Church fathers?

An attempt to redefine historic Christianity took place in many churches during the 19th and 20th centuries. But efforts to replace or confuse Christian doctrines with non-biblical teachings are not just part of the recent past; they are recorded all through Church history.

The Christian Church was established upon the firm presupposition that God revealed Himself to man in history and that this revelation was recorded in the divinely inspired writings of the Bible. If this is true then "Christian" beliefs cannot just be concocted out of thin air. If God has spoken truthfully and with authority, as claimed by the writers of Christian scripture, then how would it be possible to justify truth-claims that contradict the scripture?

The Bible clearly teaches God as the highest authority, and depicts His Word as being self-attesting. Those who claim to be Christians should presuppose the *whole* Bible is God's Word upon its *own authority*. There can be no competing sources of authority from which professing Christians can legitimately draw their conceptions of God, man, or the cosmos.

Only a *biblically-based* Christian theology can serve as an authoritative foundation for Christian beliefs because it is upon the authority of the Christian scripture as God's Word that the church was founded.[24] The Church's orthodox beliefs are rooted in the Bible's many distinctive truth-claims.

In biblical Christianity God is not a thing, power, or influence. God is not some kind of impersonal force or mind. The God of the Bible is a personal being, meaning that He is self-conscious, intelligent, and possesses self-determination. (Ex 3:14, 20:2; Jn 14:9)

Historic Christianity has taught that there is one God. This oneness refers to His unity. His "divine nature is undivided and indivisible."[25] (Deut 4: 35-39, 6:4; 1 Ki 8:60; Jn 17:3) Yet this unity does not mean "singleness. The unity of God allows for the existence of three personal distinctions in the divine nature, while at the same time recognizing that the divine nature is numerically and eternally one."[26] The three personal distinctions are co-substantial, co-dependent and co-eternal persons. God is Triune. (Gen 1:26; 3:22; Matt 3:16; 2 Cor 13:14)

The Bible reveals that God is absolute. This means, "He is sufficient unto Himself."[27] God is not "dependent upon anything outside of his being."[28] (Ex 3:14; Jn 5:26) God is the sovereign and Supreme Being. There is no higher or more authoritative being. (Ps 103:19) He is all powerful, meaning that He can do anything that does not contradict His divine nature. (Gen 18:14; Job 42:2; Matt 19:26) God owns everything in the universe (Gen 14:19; 1Chr 29:11), including all people. (Ps 24:1)

God is all-knowing. He knows everything intuitively and He cannot add to his knowledge because all facts in creation are what they are because of Him. (Ps 136:5; Ps 147:4-5; Prov 3:19-20; Heb 4:13) God is eternal. He is without beginning and without end. He has always existed. (Deut 33:27; Job 36:26; Ps 93:2) He does not change. (Mal 3:6) God is free from sin and moral imperfection. He is holy. (Isa 6:3-5)

God is the creator. He created the material universe and everything in it. He created it *ex nihlo* (out if nothing) and *ex materia* (without using any pre-existing materials). The Bible does not explain *how* God did this, only that He did do it. (Gen 1:1; Ex

20:11; Neh 9:6; Heb 11:3) God is not anything in the creation nor is anything in the creation God. God's essence is not physical. The creation itself is not God. He is distinct from His creation. His essence is incorporeal and immaterial. He does not have a physical body. God is Spirit. (Jn 4:24)

God is omnipresent, meaning that he is not subject to the limitations of space. "God is neither included in space nor absent from it. God is above all space and yet present in every part of it. (1 Ki 8:27; Acts 17:27)"[29] Christian scripture reveals that God is transcendent. This does not mean that God is far away in a spatial sense, but rather that He is not bound or restrained by the created order in any way. In other words, God transcends creation. He is Lord over it. Because of this transcendence God can invade His creation at will. Scripture also portrays God's immanence when it depicts Him as being near and intimately involved with His creation. (Ps 139:3-11; Jer 23:23-24)

God upholds and sustains all things by the word of His power. (Heb 1:3) Nothing in creation operates upon its own independent power or ability. God providentially controls all things. There is no such thing as Fate, Chance, Fortune, Luck, Mother Nature or Natural Law (impersonal laws of nature) - there is only the Providence of God. The order and arrangement of the universe are subject to and governed by His eternal decree.

All of reality reflects God's divine will and sovereign purposes. This would include *"that work of God by which He cooperates with all His creatures and causes them to act precisely as they do. It implies that there are real secondary causes in the world, such as the powers of nature and the will of man, and asserts that these do not work independently of God."*[30] (Deut 8:18; 1Sam 2:6-8; Ps 104:20-30; Isa 46:4-10; Amos 3:6; Matt 5:45, 10:29; Acts 14:17; Eph 1:11; Phil 2:13; Col 1:16-17)

Man is revealed to be a finite creature. Man has been created. God created man in His image, meaning that certain godly attributes were communicated to man within the limitations of his finite creaturehood. God's relationship to the creation is determined by His being. God did not communicate all of His attributes to man. Man is not God. Man was created as a spiritual, personal, moral, and rational being. Man's being and knowledge are completely derived from and dependent upon God who is his source. (Gen 1:26-27, 2:7, 5:1; 1Cor 15:47-49; Col 3:10; Ja 3:9)

By virtue of his being created in the image of God, man is an ethical creature. But ethical judgments were not to be made apart from the revelation given him by His Creator. "Man was to gather up in his consciousness all the meaning that God had deposited in the universe and be the reflector of it all. The revelation of God was deposited in the whole creation, but it was in the mind of man alone that this revelation was to come to self-conscious re-interpretation. Man was to be God's re-interpreter, that is, God's prophet on earth."[31] "Man shall not live by bread alone, but by every word that proceeds out of the mouth of God." (Matt 4:3)

It is not within the scope of man's creaturehood to construct ethical standards himself. Yet this is exactly what man did as Adam and Eve in the fall – and continues to do. God's prohibition to man not to partake of the "tree of the knowledge of good and evil" in the garden was not a directive against man seeking knowledge per se; it was a prohibition against man autonomously deciding for himself the difference between good and evil. "This, then, is the essence of sin; man's rebellion against recognizing his dependence on God in everything and the assumption of his ability to be independent of God."[32]

Man's autonomy means that as a creature he wants to rule himself apart from God's sovereign authority. This same attitude is manifested whenever anyone thinks or acts in accordance with what is "right in his own eyes." (Judg 17:6) The Bible refers to this as sin or lawlessness. (1Jn 3:4) In his fallen state man does not want God to rule over him. He wants to be a law unto himself. Man's sin severed his fellowship with God. This caused man to "die" spiritually, (the word "die" here implies separation, not cessation) and later physically. (Gen 2:17, 3:19)

While some worldviews see man as basically good, the Bible portrays man as sinful. This means "Man is by nature *totally depraved*. This does not mean that every man is as bad as he can be, but that sin has corrupted every part of his nature and rendered him unable to do any spiritual good. He may still do many praiseworthy things in relation to his fellow-beings, but even his best works are *radically defective*, because they are not prompted by love to God nor done in obedience to God."[33] Thus, man himself cannot remedy the sinful condition. "Your virtues can never cancel your vices."[34] Man cannot save himself. (Jer 17:9; Jn 5:42; 6:44; Rom 7:18, 23-24; 1Cor 2:14; Eph 2:1-3; 2Tim 3:2-4; Heb 11:6)

God, in His mercy, provides a remedy for the sinful condition through Christ's atoning sacrifice on the cross. This is the central theme of the Bible. It is the story about God's redemption of fallen man by pardoning man's sin in Christ. (Rom 5:19; Rom 8:30; Heb 9:14; Eph 1:10-11) In essence, the guiltless party pays the price for the guilty party. This is recognized as a beautiful story of God's love and mercy by Christians but to those who reject the Bible's gospel message it is a story of foolishness. (1 Cor 1:18)

The New Testament emphasizes Christ's atoning work, where he "fully satisfied the justice of His Father; and purchased, not only reconciliation, but an everlasting inheritance in the kingdom of heaven, for all those whom the Father has given unto Him."[35] When a believer confesses Christ as "Lord" (Rom 10:9) they find forgiveness for their sins, including their autonomous reasoning against God. (Mk 10:45; Jn 1:29; 1Pet 2:24; 1Jn 2:2)

Given the corruption of man's nature it is easy for the believer to see why the Bible's revelation of both God and man offends people. Scripture's emphasis upon the reality of sin and its consequences are truths that challenge the autonomy everyone seeks to exercise in their life. But since human beings were made in the image of God the Bible says each of us intuitively know these truths but suppress them in our inner consciousness. (Rom 1:18)

Because man is finite, his mind cannot be regarded as either the beginning or final reference point for truth. In contrast to autonomous thinking, the Christian is admonished to have the "mind of Christ" (1 Cor 2:16), and set aside "all thoughts that exalt themselves against the knowledge of God." (2 Cor 10:5) Instead of entertaining notions about God, humanity or the cosmos that contradict the Bible, all men are called to presuppose God's Word as the foundational "rock" of truth for understanding all things. (Matt 7:24-25) All knowledge, truth and wisdom are found in Christ. (1Cor 1:24, 30)

If this biblical picture of reality is true then all opposing views are false. (Deut 4:39) For example, monistic views, which teach that reality consists of one great universal whole without distinctions, are mistaken. Pantheistic views that essentially teach "god is all and all is god" cannot possibly be correct. Polytheistic views portraying the existence of many gods are wrong. Deists who believe that some type of god created the universe only to step back from it and set natural laws in motion to control and sustain it are in error. (Jer 10:10) Professing agnostics who claim that God cannot really be known to exist are inaccurate. Atheists who insist that God does not exist are incorrect. (Ps 14:1) This is not being mean spirited. It is simply logical to state that multitudinous views espousing opposite truth claims cannot all be true.

Those who hold non-Christian views will reject the Bible's truth-claims. This is because they are presupposing another metaphysical view of reality. Philosophical neutrality does not exist. Everyone favors one particular view of reality over another. Although most people may never self-consciously identify or categorize their metaphysical views they still have them nonetheless. And they will use them as a standard to judge the truth-claims recorded in the Bible.

5

Pseudo-Christianity

There is a tremendous amount of controversy among academics over how much of the archeological evidence actually reflects the Bible's accuracy as an historical source. A few scholars would say that, "Archeology has not produced anything that is unequivocally a contradiction to the Bible."[36] Others would likely side with another scholar who said, "We find a great deal in the Bible, it's just that we don't find the Bible to be a historical record."[37] Still others would position themselves somewhere in the middle.

How is it possible for such highly educated people to arrive at such different conclusions regarding the Bible's historical record? Perhaps their archeological data isn't the same, but what is almost certain is that each one is interpreting the evidence differently. Debates over how the Bible's truth-claims should be approached basically come down to one essential difference between orthodox Christianity and modern Christian liberalism. Liberal interpreters are unwilling to *presuppose* that God has authoritatively and infallibly revealed Himself through the various types of genre recorded in the Bible as the scripture itself declares.

The modern branch of biblical scholarship known as Higher Criticism, for example, rejects the idea of studying the Bible according to the claims of its writers. Historically, most biblical scholars had believed that "hermeneutics must always adapt itself to the class of literature to which it is applied."[38] But these liberal theologians present the Bible "as a disjointed collection of misleading documents, deliberately revised and rewritten by 'redactors' and editors years or even centuries later than the texts initially appear to have been written."[39]

Higher critics "interpret the Bible from within the presuppositions of the contemporary scientific worldview. Such a worldview assumes that all historical events are capable of being explained by other known historical events. In other words, what we call the supernatural is not the immediate activity of the living God; for it belongs to the area of legend and myth and not to the area of historical reality."[40] Their worldview leads them to an anti-orthodox bias before they study biblical texts. This "modern attitude can be attributed to a predisposed denial of revelation and supernaturalism, or to personal dislike for many of the concepts of Scripture."[41]

Many individuals often accept the notion that the Bible *may* contain *some* truths or facts from history but they will not accept *all of the Bible's claims based upon its own authority.* "The authority of scripture comes from God Himself – it is a self-attesting authority".[42] From an interpreter's perspective there is no higher authority to which the Bible appeals in order to validate its claims. "The Bible, skeptics insist, is at best a human book about God, and, as such, may be criticized like other human books. The evangelical too, believes that the Bible is a human book, but that it is also, and more fundamentally, a divine book and is to be so treated. The two approaches therefore end up poles apart."[43]

Those who penned the books of the Bible presented their works as both *divinely inspired* and *true* accounts of God and His dealings with man. This includes the supra-natural events described within biblical literature. Bible-believers assume that while God chose to involve man in the process, there was "special divine influence on the minds of the writers of the Bible, in virtue of which their productions, apart from errors in transcription, and when rightly interpreted, together constitute an infallible rule of faith and practice."[44] This belief is at the heart of Christianity's affirmation that the sixty-six books of the Bible are the Word of God.

The Bible appeals to no authority other than itself and claims to be the very Word of God. Either it is or it is not. If it is then it must be taken on its own authority and accepted as God's revelation to man. The Apostles claimed that all scripture is completely inspired of God, (2 Tim 3:16) authoritative, (Matt 5:17-19) and true in what it records. (1Thess 2:13) This includes its entire picture of reality, including propositions about God, man and the cosmos.

Christian scholarship has produced large amounts of historical, scientific and archeological data over the years that show much of the biblical record may be corroborated with extra-biblical sources of information. Such scholarship is perfectly legitimate. But the people, places and events recorded in the Bible cannot be separated from its underlying metaphysical view of reality. "For every critic – the liberal just as much as the evangelical – establishing limits is a matter of faith, either in one's own internal competence, or in another's (Christ's) external authority."[45] It is impossible to use isolated or independent facts to conclude the Bible is what it claims to be. This should not come as a surprise to anyone who claims to be a Christian.

If special revelation was communicated to man by God then it is reasonable to assume there might be things within it that may not appear to be logical (to man's finite reason), scientific (given man's limited understanding of the natural world), or historically verifiable (due to man's incomplete knowledge of the past). It would also mean that whatever might appear to be contradictions in the Bible must be just that - apparent but not actual. Scripture contends that God does not contradict himself. (2 Cor 1:18) In the Christian view, all apparent discrepancies could, in fact, be resolved if finite man could gather enough information regarding the details in question. However, the metaphysical limitations of man's finite being prevent this possibility.

As a finite creature it is impossible for man to gather the comprehensive knowledge that would be necessary in order to accept *some* of what the Bible teaches about God while rejecting other truths set forth in that same Bible. Man's reason is finite and therefore limited. Finite creatures cannot know universal truths apart from a source of universal knowledge. Contriving so-called "Christian" doctrines with personally pre-conceived or supplemented ideas about the God of Christianity is theologically illegitimate. Such ideas are the basis for heterodox Christian truth-claims. Yet how can such claims be asserted by *professing Christians* in light of the Bible's claims of divine inspiration and inerrancy? If God has in fact spoken to man in the Bible then what has been revealed must be taken on its own authority without adding to it or subtracting from it. (Rev 22:18-19)

Theologians and philosophers of Christian liberalism have ended up creating their own interpretive obstacles by their abandonment of historic Christianity in favor of manmade pseudo-Christianity. "What higher critics want us to believe in is the world according to Immanuel Kant, a dialectical realm composed of two utterly separate worlds: the phenomenal world of historical facts – meaningless historical facts apart from man's interpretations of them – and the trans-historical noumenal world of human meaning – utterly timeless, non-cognitive meaning – that is completely distinct from the phenomenal world of cause and effect".[46]

Liberal scholars have tried to "demythologize"[47] many of the Bible's claims only to later "adopt the language of praise, telling readers that, while mythical, the Bible is nevertheless a majestic document that deserves an important place in the varied and complex history of man's religions.

In short, as hoaxes go, the Bible is a good one, as good or better than all the other hoaxes in man's religious history."[48] If this liberal view of scripture were correct then non-Christians would be fully justified to ask whether or not the Bible really has any type of divine inspiration or meaning to it at all.

It is nonsense to argue that the Bible is spiritually relevant to man while simultaneously professing that it contains many factual

errors whenever any of its details touch history or science. If human beings simply conjured up Christianity's origin then it is really nothing more than an existential leap of faith. Honesty would demand of
Christians to admit they are embracing an unverifiable hope that is disconnected from the reality of the natural world.

The difference between Christian orthodoxy and liberalism is perhaps best demonstrated in how each group approaches the book of Genesis. Evangelicals view this book as an historical record of literal events. Modern liberals present it as either a collection of allegorical stories mixed with some verifiable ancient history or as a largely mythological tale. This reflects the liberals' "widespread tendency ...to treat historiography as another genre of fiction."[49] The problem with this, of course, is that to read Genesis as anything other than literal time-space history completely calls into question whether or not any Christian scripture contains truth.

It is impossible to take any parts of the Bible seriously, including the New Testament, if the historical accounts in the Old Testament are not true. "It is safe to say that in no recorded utterance of Jesus and in no written or spoken statement of his apostles is there any suggestion of scientific or historical inaccuracy in any Old Testament record."[50] Christianity itself stands upon what is written in the Old Testament. "Christ himself believed in the infallibility of scripture, and, if he was wrong in that belief, by what means can we know he was right in any other?"[51]

If the historicity and verity of Genesis cannot be relied upon then many New Testament passages, such as the following ones are not just brought into question, they become completely unintelligible.

- Christ's death, burial, and resurrection are presented by the Apostle Paul as the remedy for the problem of a human sinful condition originating in the person of Adam. (Rom 5:14; 1Cor 15:22, 45)

• The serpent's deception of Eve in the garden is referenced as an example of the same kind of spiritual warfare faced by all believers. (2Cor 11:3)

• The institution of marriage has its beginnings in the historical relationship of Adam and Eve, (1Tim 2:13-14) which also serves as a type of Christ's relationship to His church. (Ephes 5:23)

• Jesus was born a human being with traceable Jewish genealogical lineage extending back to Adam. (Luke 3:23-38)

• Cain and Abel are Adam's literal offspring, with Cain depicted as killing his brother Abel. (Matt 23:35; Luke 11:51; Heb 11:4; Jude 11)

• The faith of Noah is set apart by his obedience to God in preparing an ark to save his family from a literal flood. (Heb 11:7; 1Pet 3:20; 2 Pet 2:5)

• The destruction of the cities of Sodom and Gomorrah are cited as factual examples of God's wrath against sin. (Jude 7; Matt 11:23 –24; Luke 17:29; Mark 6:11; Luke 10:12; 2Pet 2:6)

• Enoch is recorded to be a prophet in the seventh generation from Adam. (Jude 14)

• Christians are identified as heirs of Abraham's covenant with God because believers in Christ are considered to be Abraham's spiritual offspring. (Romans 9; Gal 3:29)

If these events did not actually happen as they are recorded in Genesis then readers are left with many unanswerable questions. If man's fall into sin through the person of Adam is not an historical event then does *sin* really exist? If so, then how did it *enter* the human race? Did Jesus himself *know* that many of the stories in Genesis were only allegorical or mythological? Was the Apostle Paul mistaken (or deceptive) by proclaiming that Jesus Christ personally appeared to him and revealed that he was God who came in the flesh to remedy Adam's sin? Why does Paul refer to Christ as the second Adam? Was the resurrection of Christ a literal time-space event as the apostles claimed? If not, then what significance could it possibly have with the real world?

The *continuity* of the Bible's message depends upon the collective context of *all* scriptural writings. A plenary approach to biblical scripture is required to arrive at any logical interpretation at all because scripture constantly references the truth-claims in other portions of scripture. One cannot take the parts of the Bible they like and discard what does not personally appeal to them. The Bible is not a summary of eclectic spiritual thoughts. Christianity is not a smorgasbord type of belief system where individuals can take "a little of this or a little of that". The Bible must be taken as a whole. It's all or nothing. Disregarding certain portions of scripture in favor of others cannot be done unless the Bible is not what it claims to be – the revealed Word of God.

Christian liberalism also seems to ignore the fact that moral claims need to be based upon some kind of authority. The Bible's moral claims are based upon the historical contention that God actually spoke to man. The Ten Commandments are based upon the authority from which they are derived. If they were merely conjured up by man then they really are not universally binding moral principles. They are just one set of opinions among many. Thinking skeptics will gladly point this out.

It is amazing how many so-called "scholars" will lecture about the meaningfulness of scripture after they have worked so hard to deconstruct its language in an effort to "debunk" its historical claims. But this kind of approach does not hold objective truth for anyone – especially liberals. Liberals want us to believe that the Bible's own historical framework, grammar and syntax cannot be trusted to convey objective meaning yet liberals are somehow able to know the *real meaning* behind the words using their own finite human reason.

If the Bible is what it claims to be then man must conform his views to those of God, his Creator. We are instructed to think God's thoughts after Him. (Isa 55:9) This requires a presuppositional approach to scripture. Believers must begin their reasoning with the truths revealed in the Bible because they take it on its own authority to be God's Word.

> The Bible is thought of as authoritative on everything of which it speaks. And *it speaks of everything*. We do not mean that it speaks of football games, of atoms, etc., directly, but we do mean that it speaks of everything either directly or indirectly. It tells us not only of Christ and his work but it also tells us who God is and whence the universe has come. It gives us a philosophy of history as well as history. Moreover, the information on these subjects is woven into an inextricable whole. It is only if you reject the Bible as the Word of God that you can separate its so-called religious and moral instruction from what it says, e.g., about the physical universe.[52]

Jesus is portrayed in many unbiblical ways today. These portrayals of him convey a skewered picture of who Jesus really was. The liberals' rejection of the doctrines of divine inspiration and biblical inerrancy opens the door for them to try and remake the Christology reflected within Christendom's ancient creeds. But re-defining the person of Christ apart from what the scriptures actually teach about him is nothing more than positing metaphysical Christian truth absent of any legitimate authority.

Many liberals have simply *fabricated* the kind of Jesus they *want* to believe in. This construction of new biblical doctrine, especially within once mainline denominations, is nothing less than old-fashioned heresy. The Bible itself records that there were false teachings about Christ being spread during Christianity's early days in the ancient world. The apostles dealt squarely with these false doctrines in their epistles to the church. They used both the Old Testament and their eyewitness testimonies as God's spokesman to authoritatively establish doctrinal truth. The apostle Paul warned Galatian believers about those who came proclaiming a gospel of Christ different from the one he had preached to them. (Gal 1:6-9) There was only one genuine gospel of Jesus Christ, not many.

The Bible is an Eastern book recorded against the background of ancient history. Because of this we can understand why its readers often have sincere questions regarding the meaning of particular passages. But it is one thing for someone to question the meaning of scriptures that are *revealing truth* and another thing entirely to look for meaning in the Bible even though many things it records *are not true*.

A Christianity where God has not revealed both Himself and His inerrant truth to man via the special revelation of scripture can be neither rationally defined nor defended. The design-your-own-god-and-lifestyle type of Christianity popular among many today does not have any basis in the scriptures. It may emphasize "good works" (however one chooses to define "good") or encourage benevolent activities, but it is not biblical Christianity, and it should not be referred to as "Christian".

6

Knowing Biblical Christianity Is True

The evidence required to prove something exists must correspond to its *nature*. For example, the evidence offered as proof for the existence of gravity is not the same kind that is used to prove a mathematical theory. In the same way, proof for God's existence corresponds to what the Bible reveals about the nature of His Being.

Since the Bible reveals that God is not a part of the physical universe then He cannot be seen with the physical eye nor can his existence be verified through scientific investigation. Those holding a materialistic view of the universe will object to this, of course, because they presuppose that reality is composed essentially of matter and energy. Thus materialism in and of itself amounts to an *a priori53* rejection of the God of the Bible.

Since non-Christian worldviews contain presuppositions that differ from those in the Christian worldview, the disagreements about whether or not Christianity is true involve much more than dispute over certain facts. Questions involving God's existence as well as what kind of God He is will always involve a *worldview conflict* between the Christian and non-Christian. Can such a dispute be resolved to any satisfactory conclusion? The answer is yes.

The history of philosophy represents man's efforts to explain the most significant questions in life by beginning with his own finite mind as a reference point for truth. The Greek philosopher Protagoras expressed this method of defining absolutes using autonomous human reason by saying that, "man is the measure of all things." "For most modern people, the conscious or unconscious starting point is their own existence and their own reason...People thus start from themselves, and assume that only their own human reason can decide whether something is true."54 This approach to finding truth is inadequate because man is not big enough to do the measuring.

> From the beginning, man has forgotten that he is finite, limited, and weak. Pride prompts in us, as it did Adam and Eve, the desire to be like God, to function as God. Pride also leads us to imagine that we have enough strength and wisdom actually to play the divine role, controlling all around us with perfect mastery and glorying in the thought that there is nothing we cannot do.[55]

Since man naturally assumes his autonomous human reason "to be the final reference point in predication"[56] he is faced with an ever-present philosophical dilemma. It is simply taken for granted that "man, beginning totally independently and autonomously, can build a bridge towards ultimate truth – as if attempting to build a cantilever bridge out from himself across an infinite gorge. This is not possible, because man is finite and, as such, he has nothing toward which he can point with certainty. He has no way, beginning from himself, to set up sufficient universals."[57]

Because man is an individual, finite, and limited creature, certainty of knowledge using this approach would require a person to know *everything* before they could truly know *anything*. But infinite knowledge is not possible for finite beings. It is impossible, epistemologically speaking, for man to use himself as a reference point for truth. Man's limited mind cannot be used as an ultimate standard.

Recognizing that "man cannot generate final answers from himself"[58] should help one to comprehend that this knowledge problem is solved if absolute truth has come to mankind from God.

The Bible comes to man as just such a revelation of truth from the infinite God to His finite creature, presenting its truth-claims from within this context. Christians believe that God has spoken truthfully, although not exhaustively, in scripture. They take the Bible at face value with respect to what it teaches about God's work in the universe and His historical dealings with man.

> It must be acknowledged that human knowledge is always relative to the knower, and is always based on that human being's experience and presuppositions, but (there is an important distinction between knowing an absolute truth and knowing a truth absolutely). Humans can know an absolute, transcendent truth if that truth is known by an absolute Person whose knowledge does *not* depend on experience and if that absolute Person shares His knowledge with humans. It is a conviction, indeed a basic assumption, of the biblical writers that such a Person indeed is there and that He has communicated truth in Scripture. Scripture writers assume God is there and that He has spoken. Thus we may know absolute truth, albeit not absolutely; we may know it truly, even though only partially and imperfectly. The atheist or agnostic may cry "presupposition" at us, but we may point out that they are presupposing that God has not spoken.[59]

In a Christian worldview the exercise of human reason in pursuit of knowledge first assumes that man's logic is a reflection of the mind of God. As a creature created in God's image, man was also endowed with the ability to reason logically. This ability, although finite, points back to man's Creator. Logic did not originate within an abstract mind floating around somewhere in the universe. God is the source of all reasoning and in order for man to reason properly his finite logic must rely upon God's infallible revelation as an ultimate reference point for truth.

> The Christian…affirms the validity of human reason, but maintains that it can only have a proper ground if we acknowledge first that God the Creator exists, that He has communicated with humanity, and that He constituted our "reason" as an effective tool for comprehension of language and all else in the created world. This Christian starting point is not a groundless assumption. According to Romans 1:19-21, all human beings are constituted such that they know the essential attributes of God, because the creation screams at them that it, and they themselves, have been made by God.[60]

Genesis tells us that even in the Garden of Eden God talked with man and gave him revelation through His spoken Word prior to the fall. (Gen 2:16-17) In the Christian view "all the thinker's in the world will never conceive independently the secrets of life, origins, and destiny…they only come by revelation."[61]

At the very heart of a Christian's profession of faith is a renouncement of the intellectual autonomy that was at the center of man's fall into sin. The change of mind whereby a Christian renounces his intellectual self-sufficiency in favor of presupposing truths found in scripture is known as repentance. Man's sin during the Fall was illustrated in his putting God's Word to the test. As a finite creature man is forbidden to test God's Word. (Luke 4:12) Instead God calls man to believe Him. Man is to take God at His Word and not reason against it.

What most people want to do is judge the Bible according to their finite reason. They want the Bible to appeal to their own "logic." An example of this is when skeptics demand to fully know how the existence of a supposedly good God comports with the existence of evil. Others refuse to accept eternal justice allowing for the existence of an eternal hell. But what these self-appointed "judges" of scripture neglect to confront themselves with are questions of ultimacy such as, "What type of reality must exist in order for logic, evil, or justice to exist in the first place?"

The Bible connects man's ability to obtain true knowledge with the reality of God's existence. (Prov 1:7, 9:10) Scripture references knowledge with respect to God because it teaches that God's Being is a prerequisite for man's ability to reason and achieve knowledge. "God's understanding of Himself and the creation is independent but man's knowledge is dependent. The Psalmist put it this way: In thy light we see light (Ps. 36:9)...Men do actually think, yet, true knowledge is dependent on and derived from God's knowledge as it has been revealed to man."[62] God's Word is presented as the "light" that opens up our understanding. This light is the necessary prerequisite no matter what area of life we are attempting to discover or understand.

The Bible never separates so-called "spiritual" truths from "secular" ones. On the contrary, the Apostle Paul emphasized that "all wisdom and knowledge" is contained in the revelation of Christ, who is God in the flesh. (Col 2:3) The Bible contends that "all wisdom and knowledge is deposited in the person of Christ - whether it be about the War of 1812, water's chemical composition, the literature of Shakespeare, or the laws of logic. Every academic pursuit and every thought must be related to Jesus Christ, for Jesus is the way, *the truth*, and the life. (Jn 14:6)"[63] How is this so?

The many worldviews found in this earth reflect very diverse conceptions of reality. "Presuppositions form the basis of the 'interpretive framework' by which we understand things."[64] Each belief system portrays ideas about God, man and the world in very different ways. Every belief system shows so-called facts in a different "light" of understanding than another one does. Facts are not viewed the same by those who hold differing worldviews. Our worldview not only provides us with a picture of what is real, it also dictates how we think we know that it is real. To put it another way, our epistemology (how we think we know what we know) is directly tied to our metaphysic (what we conceive to be real).

Scripture teaches that in order to obtain knowledge about man, science, ethics, the cosmos or to interpret any aspect of human experience the truths God has revealed to man in both creation and scripture *must be presupposed.* The Christian presuppositions discussed in chapter four are not merely abstract theological beliefs. The Bible teaches they are collectively essential to man's interpretation of reality. *In principle*, they are required assumptions that must be relied upon if one is to have any type of knowledge at all. Biblical truths must be presupposed because they alone provide "the preconditions of intelligibility for man's reasoning, experience and dignity."[65]

Christianity is proven true by the "impossibility of the contrary."[66] Only a Christian worldview rooted in the Bible, taken as God's Word, provides a sure basis for knowing (epistemology). Christianity demands our intellectual commitment because only the biblical worldview can *account for* true knowledge.

In the course of religious discussion between Christians and non-Christians *both* sides should be put into the position of justifying their beliefs. To reason against Christianity one must do more than simply deny it. *Adherents of other belief systems must also justify their own faith-based presuppositions about reality.* This is the heart of the matter. Christians can justifiably claim that absolute certain proof of Christianity is possible because only the Christian belief system offers the foundational premises necessary for rational thought and discourse.

According to scripture all people have a genuine knowledge of God that comes from His self-revelation in creation. (Rom 1:18-

21; Acts 17:27-28) Although most people may deny having this knowledge, scripture teaches that man not only has it, but also seeks to suppress it. As God's image bearer, man cannot logically reflect upon himself, the human condition or any fact without revealing that he does in fact possess such knowledge. Those who do not hold to a biblical view of reality must inevitably "borrow" from the biblical worldview even though they reject biblical theology. "Those who do not know God only 'know' on borrowed capital; they really do know things, but only because they are made in God's image. They have no justification for their knowledge."[67] *While they deny the Christian metaphysic in principal they operate upon it in the real world out of necessity.*

Though man works to suppress his knowledge of God with other worldviews *only the Christian worldview* provides human beings with a basis for realities such as the laws of logic, dignity of man, regularities of nature and ethical absolutes. These things do not independently exist apart from any meaningful cause. Their existence is contingent upon the existence of the God of the Bible and His sovereign arrangement of the universe as revealed in scripture. Non-Christian worldviews cannot account for the human freedom, science, morality or tools of reason exercised in productive life and meaningful human experience. The Bible *makes its own case* by providing the only possible unifying principle for all areas of knowledge – the Triune God Himself.

> ...therefore the claim must be made that Christianity alone is reasonable for men to hold. And it is utterly reasonable. It is wholly irrational to hold to any other position than that of Christianity. Christianity alone does not crucify reason itself. Without it reason would operate in a total vacuum...with Augustine it must be maintained that God's revelation is the sun from which all other light derives. The best, the only, the absolutely certain proof of the truth of Christianity is that unless its truth be presupposed there is no proof

of anything. Christianity is proved as being the very foundation of the idea of proof itself.[68]

Knowledge of science, ethics and man is rooted in a Christian view of reality. Non-Christian views, however, will "oppose themselves." (2 Tim 2:25) Their fundamental beliefs will fail to properly integrate with one other. Their systems will be either inherently contradictory or their presuppositions will fail to account for man's knowledge and experience. By relying upon the Bible's truth-claims as a necessary foundation for epistemology Christians may demonstrate that non-Christian systems are proven false at their foundational level. The metaphysical reality revealed in the Bible must be held as true because only such a reality can account for man truly "knowing" anything at all.

7

Do Christians Reason In a Circle?

Skeptics often accuse Christians of adopting the Bible's faith-view so they can escape from the "fact" that man is on his own in a random, chance universe. They see Christianity as a pie-in-the-sky outlook often embraced by those who are not bold enough to shape their own lives and world into something better. Could it be there is even something about the human condition, perhaps the fear of death, which motivates certain people into wanting Christianity to be true?

What must be pointed out is that such thinking can be applied to the skeptic as easily as the Christian. Isn't it equally valid for the believer to ask why someone may *not want* Christianity to be true? Changing worldviews involves changing the way we look at every aspect of life and reality. How much personal pride or selfish desire may be intermingled within a life-view we may have spent years constructing for ourselves?

> For myself, as, no doubt, for most of my contemporaries, the philosophy of meaninglessness was essentially an instrument of liberation. The liberation we desired was simultaneously liberation from a certain political and economic system and liberation from a certain system of morality. We objected to the morality because it interfered with our sexual freedom...I had motives for not wanting the world to have meaning; consequently I assumed that it had none, and was able without any difficulty to find satisfying reasons for this assumption. Most ignorance is vincible ignorance. We don't know because we don't want to know. It is our

will that decides how and upon what subjects we shall use our intelligence.[69]

In the preceding quote, atheist Aldous Huxley admitted that non-Christians might have certain underlying motives for embracing their particular worldview. Everyone should acknowledge that subjective preferences, emotions or personal biases are not valid reasons for determining whether or not something is true. Most people have certain beliefs they hold to very sincerely. But sincerity does not replace the need for one's faith to correspond with facts and reason. It is possible to be *sincerely wrong* about what we believe. Worldviews need to be truth-tested. Yet this immediately raises a question. What is the proper standard we must use in order to truth-test worldviews?

Once again, we are faced with the undeniable fact that our worldview is rooted in faith. Each one of us *assumes* the ultimate metaphysical yardstick by which we measure any claims made about reality. Both the Christian and Non-Christian have their presuppositions. Every person's worldview is built upon some set of non-negotiable assumptions. There are no *neutral* presuppositions. The criterion we use to judge whether or not another view is true is contained *within* our present worldview. Those who hold non-Christian presuppositions will embrace *an authority other than the Bible* by faith.

Many people insist that there is a logical problem with Christian believers operating upon the basic assumptions that God does in fact exist and that the Bible is His authoritative Word. After all they ask, do not these assumptions beg the very questions under consideration? Do Christians reason in a circle if they assume Christianity is true in order to prove Christianity is true?

There is no question that Christianity does, in fact, presuppose God's existence as described within the Bible to try and make a case for the truth-claims found within those very same scriptures. But one must not forget that this is true of *all other worldviews* as well. It is no more illegitimate for the Christian to presuppose God's existence than it is for the non-Christian to assume his non-existence.

Everyone accepts certain starting points in their thinking. Our presuppositions establish the boundaries of what we consider to be possible. They set the limits of what we will accept as evidence for proof or reject as non-evidence. Christians presuppose biblical truth as the ultimate standard by which they test other views. This is simply being consistent with the Christian belief system, since the Bible claims to be the authoritative Word of God.

Man is not permitted to test God's Word with his finite reasoning. (Deut. 6:16) Since God's Word is *ultimate* authority then scripture can only be tested with *other scripture*. Obedience to scripture's mandate requires Christians to exercise faithfulness in their reasoning. We must assume that God exists as revealed in the Bible, and then measure its claims against its own authority.

This circumstance is not unique to Christianity. *Everyone* claims to know whether something is true or not by measuring it against some kind of assumed standard within their existing belief system. For example, empiricists believe that knowledge is derived from experience, whether of the physical senses or mind. This is why the empiricist will accept scientific investigation as a valid method to prove that something is real. Rationalists, on the other hand, assume that human reason alone serves as the ultimate standard for knowledge. The rationalist will point to knowledge of logic, mathematics, and ethics to show that knowledge can be obtained apart from experience. In each case the individual's worldview determines the standard used to truth-test other views. Everyone is in the position of *assuming* an ultimate standard in order to *prove* that self-same standard.

Ultimate standards are *self-attesting*. Ultimate standards for truth must be permitted to stand (or fall) on their own. There is no logical problem with Christians accepting the authority of the Bible upon its own testimony as God's Word. If the Bible is God's very own Word then His Word would be the ultimate standard for truth and there could not possibly be any other authority used to test it. *Lesser* authorities cannot be used to test *greater* authorities.

> Whether one's theory of knowledge is grounded in demonstrative reasoning, common sense, or something else, this, and not scripture becomes the ultimate authority of the one who adheres to it. It becomes more sure than the sure Word of God. The scripture teaches us that scripture itself is to be our authority (2 Pet 1:19, 21; 2 Tim 3:16, 17; 1 John 5:9; 1 Thess 2:13). If scripture is the final authority, and if one proves the authority of scripture on the basis of something else other than scripture, then one proves the scripture is not the final authority. In other words, to prove the authority of scripture on something other than scripture is to disprove scripture.[70]

If it is wrong for Christians to presuppose what the Bible claims to be then it is just as wrong for those who hold contrary views to arbitrarily adopt standards they assume are self-validating. Worldviews are not neutral and everyone who judges the Bible's credibility will scrutinize it with the basic beliefs contained within their own worldview. So if each of us regard the presuppositions within our worldview as ultimate then those presuppositions will have to *justify themselves* in the end.

Christianity's truth-claims ultimately rest upon the authority of the scripture itself. The Bible must stand on its own testimony. The fact that one's belief system may allow for historical accuracy in some parts of the biblical record does not prove the Bible is the very Word of God. Even if every natural detail of the Bible could be corroborated with extra-biblical, historical or archeological evidence there still would not be any way to empirically authenticate all of its metaphysical assertions or justify the writers' interpretations. To prove certain isolated biblical facts does not validate biblical

Christianity as a *belief system*. Only by taking the *whole* Bible (including its integrated history-theology) and demonstrating it to be *the absolute standard necessary for interpreting all of reality* (as it claims) can it be proven true.

When it comes to their ultimate standards, both the Christian and the non-Christian reason in a circle. It is critical to understand, however, that "Christian circularity and non-Christian circularity are radically different. The former provides the fulfillment of man's purpose on earth, and the latter throws the unbeliever into a whirl of inconsistencies and self-contradictions."[71]

> Indeed, it is the case, as many will be quick to point out, that this presuppositional method of apologetics assumes the truth of scripture in order to argue for the truth of scripture. Such is unavoidable when ultimate truths are being debated. However, such is not damaging, for it is not a flat circle in which one reasons (i.e., " the Bible is true because the Bible is true"). Rather, the Christian apologist simply recognizes that the ultimate truth - that which is more pervasive, fundamental, and necessary – is such that it cannot be argued independently of the pre-conditions inherent in it. One must presuppose the truth of God's revelation in order to reason at all – even when reasoning about God's revelation. The fact that the apologist presupposes the Word of God in order to carry on a discussion or to debate about the veracity of that word does not nullify his argument, but rather illustrates it.[72]

It is not possible for anyone, including Christians, to lay aside their most basic beliefs while attempting to justify their most basic beliefs. Everyone has certain fundamental beliefs they will not lay aside, even as they attempt to justify those very same beliefs. The Bible is presented to man as the self-attesting, self-authenticating Word of God. This assumption is at the very heart of Christianity's theology and defense of the faith. The Word of God stands upon its own authority.

8
God and Evil

One of the most frequently heard objections to the Christian faith, especially from anti-theists, is what has been referred to as the "problem of evil." The essence of this argument is that the presence of evil in this world is inconsistent with the Bible's teaching that God is both good and all-powerful. Both propositions are set forth to point out a supposed logical contradiction within Christian doctrine regarding the character of God.

Philosopher David Hume described the issue this way: "Is he willing to prevent evil, but not able? Then is he impotent. Is he able, but not willing? Then is he is malevolent."[73] Writer C. S. Lewis rephrased it: "If God were good, He would wish to make his creatures perfectly happy, and if God were almighty, He would be able to do what he wished. But the creatures are not happy. Therefore, God lacks either goodness, or power, or both."[74]

The skeptic contends that if there is a God who willingly permits evil then He could not be good. God Himself would be sadistic to permit such a thing. On the other hand, if God is not able to remove evil then He cannot be omnipotent. Either way it is impossible to rationally conclude that God can be *both* good and omnipotent in the face of evil's obvious existence. Since Christians affirm both of these characteristics are part of God's nature the question they are faced with is, "How is it possible to believe that God is both good and omnipotent in light of the fact that there is evil in the world?"

When considering this question it is important to realize that in order to discuss evil the issue must be framed within a *moral context*. This creates an immediate dilemma for the skeptic who takes evil seriously. Some type of moral framework must be assumed in the universe that can be used to determine whether or not something is "evil." Yet such a framework posits exactly the kind of reality that Christianity's opponents claim is inconsistent with the problem of evil. It turns out that evil is not a rational obstacle to the Christian faith at all. The reality of evil is actually an irrational problem for cynics.

Instead of simply taking evil's existence for granted, critics must explain evil from the perspective of their worldview. This is where anti-theists encounter significant problems with their own moral logic. The atheist "asserts that he can, by the power of unaided reason, arrive at the nature of morality and at a satisfactory moral law."[75] All human attempts to construct a moral universe apart from God fall short.

What moral framework must be posited in order to establish moral judgements? How does the anti-theist know, for example, that the tragedies experienced by so many in this world are unjust? If God does not exist the events of this world are only consequences of a random, chance universe. All events, *whether one likes them or not*, are neither good nor evil. They are simply the result of interactions between matter and energy.

Is something "good" simply because an individual decides it is good? If so, then one man's cruelty could be just as good as another's generosity. Others could not judge subjective attitudes like racism as wrong.

Does majority approval or practice determine goodness? If the majority within any culture determines ethical standards for that culture then ethical judgements about other cultures would always be wrong. There also would be no way to access whether or not a culture could be *better* than it now is because that would appeal to some standard other than that culture. Should western influences have been permitted to affect the movement to officially end the practice of widow burning in India?

Attempting to determine right from wrong by majorities also fails to distinguish between *what is* the case from what *ought to be* the case. "It is necessary to assume the ethical from the beginning in order to move from an 'is' to an 'ought'."[76] This implies there are moral principles that are higher than majority opinions or cultural standards. Just because the ancient Aztecs *did* practice child sacrifice during certain pagan rituals does not mean they *should* have practiced it.

Some people define moral rightness in terms of that which brings the greatest "good" to the "greatest number" of people. But this utilitarian answer simply begs questioning. What is "right" is just replaced by what is "good." But one is still left to ask what it means to be good? It must also be asked, "How can one possibly prescribe a moral principle, or the lack of one, without justifying the authority of the source?"[77]

The question of defining goodness in ethics is at the heart of the issue of human rights. The assumption behind human rights is that man has certain fundamental rights not even governments can violate. But all types of humanistic moral theories fail to provide the philosophical basis for universal human rights. If rights are not derived from an authority higher than the state then the value of human life and freedom of human beings are dependent upon the whims of their civil rulers. "Only when God grants rights is someone prohibited from taking them away."[78] If rights originate with man, they can be taken away by man.

Christianity teaches that moral law is rooted in the very character and nature of God. Something is not *good* because God arbitrarily wills it is good. Nor does God decree that something is good because there is some standard above Him to which He must conform. God is good, and since man has been created in God's image, man's character ought to reflect the character of his Creator. (1 Pet 1:15-16)

If the skeptic's worldview cannot *account for evil* then any charges against God's omnipotence or benevolence over the *presence of evil* in this world are meaningless. There is no moral universe without a moral standard rooted in the transcendent, unchanging character of God. Without it nothing is truly evil, and therefore, there is no problem of evil. In order to make evil an issue antagonists must *rely upon* the Christian worldview, which provides a genuine basis for evil, in order to try to *disprove* the Christian worldview.

God's existence is a precondition for the *knowledge of both good and evil*. Without God there are only non-moral, random events that occur in this world. Some of them may be personally undesirable, but they cannot be referred to as evil.

One may still ask, though, that even if evil cannot be accounted for *apart from* the Christian worldview is it not a contradiction *within* the Christian worldview? This is a genuine question, but anyone who asks it must be willing keep in mind that the Bible does not offer man a *comprehensive* answer to many questions, including this one. It does offer a *meaningful* answer within the *context* of the Christian worldview itself.

Scripture does not only refer to God as all-powerful and good. It also teaches that He is omniscient or all knowing. Man, however, has a metaphysical limitation to his knowledge. The infinite God comprehensively knows things that finite man does not know. We must accept the fact that as finite and fallen creatures we face both cognitive and moral obstacles that hinder us from fully comprehending why God has chosen, in His omniscience, to allow evil and its affects in this world.

When man approaches the subject of evil he should realize that he is himself infected with the very evil he wants to use as an issue to question the goodness of God. It is evident from scripture that God permits evil and suffering to achieve certain ends. Could these ends involve saving fallen man and effecting changes within him for his ultimate good? Can evil be something God permits in relation to man's present fallen nature for man's ultimate good?

God has elected to permit evil at this time for morally sufficient reasons known only to Him. Man is not in either an ethical or intellectual position to understand God's eternal plan for the ages. God has allowed evil to enter the world through secondary causes as part of a comprehensive plan He has only partially revealed at this time. God's ways are just and He calls upon us to live our lives by faith and trust in Him just as Adam and Eve were created to do. (Isa 45:21)

The Bible records that when Job lost his family, health, and prosperity he yearned to know why, but God did not give him the answers he sought. Instead, Job was made to realize the futility of trying to fully fathom the workings of an infinite God. He also realized that he must trust the Lord in spite of the temporal, tragic circumstances. God's Sovereignty is a biblical reality, and man's being exists in subordinate relationship to it. The presence of evil in this world is not a *logical* problem for Christianity. It is a genuine *physical* and *emotional* problem for everyone that presently lives in this world, including Christians.

It is fully consistent with the Christian worldview to believe that an infinite God has a bigger plan for man than what finite man is currently able to conceive. Though God does not share with us the reasons why He chooses to allow evil in the world at this time, He does assure us that it is a *temporal condition* in the light of eternity. Christians have a refuge and hope in the eternal promises of a God who is faithful and true to His word. They look forward to a future where evil is finally put away, and where ultimate questions are fully satisfied with the complete knowledge that can only come from God.

9

Atheism and Agnosticism

Everyone believes in some type of *ultimate* reality. Christians believe that reality begins with an infinite personal God who has revealed Himself to man in the Bible. According to scripture everything that truly exists has its point of reference in the God who created it. (Proverbs 1:7; Matthew 7:24-27) In spite of this, there are those who attempt to construct a metaphysical view that does not acknowledge the existence of God. While there are both secular and religious varieties of anti-theism the most aggressive opposition to historic Christianity in the West still comes from naturalistic atheism.

Atheism should not be confused with agnosticism. By definition atheism is the profession that God does not exist. It is an outright denial of all types of theism. Agnosticism professes that no one can really know whether or not God exists. Such opponents of the Christian worldview must face the fact that it is one thing to attack the doctrines of the Bible, but another thing altogether to defend their own basic worldview presuppositions from which they judge Christianity's teachings.

An outright denial of God's existence poses an immediate problem for someone who professes to be a hardcore atheist. The naturalistic atheist's assumptions about God's non-existence cannot be *proven* outright. Human finiteness precludes the possibility of investigating the entire cosmos to "see" whether or not God exists. An outright denial of God's existence would require one to possess infinite knowledge. A true atheistic argument is impossible. To avoid this problem most anti-theists attempt to argue that none of the world's religions offer a compelling case for belief in God. This is, in effect, a retreat to agnosticism.

The Bible teaches that all men know God exists because "the knowledge of God is inherent in man. It is there by virtue of his creation in the image of God. This may be called innate knowledge."[79] The problem is not lack of evidence but willful suppression of the evidence. (Rom 1:18)

Evidence for the existence of the Triune God is reflected through the nature and operation of self-consciousness itself. Man was fashioned in the image of God. According to Scripture man is comprised of an *inner* self as well as an outer self. The body of man has a *soul*.

The core belief of materialistic atheism is that only "material" things exist. Since this position assumes that immaterial realities are not provable in a material-only universe then immaterial realities either do not exist or cannot be known to exist. If this assumption is fundamental to the atheists' worldview then atheists must adhere to it. They must stand upon this intellectual ground to *interpret all things*, including *themselves*.

Materialistic atheism must define man's nature from supposed "natural" origins and elements. This results in a very restricted view of man. Materialism's inability to account for the intangible nature of the soul leads to an inability to either account for or make genuine distinctions between physical and mental properties within man's nature.

Immaterial states of consciousness cannot be understood in a material-only universe. Either consciousness is itself material or it is a state of being essentially generated from physical properties. However, if either one of these options is adopted then abstract free thought can only be an illusion. If our ideas and thinking processes are matter-energy impulses resulting from natural forces, then thinking is not something *we choose* to do, it's merely something the *body does* – like regulating the heartbeat or growing hair. The mental state is little more than a result of physiological and chemical reactions within human anatomy. The notion of free thought and its use in reason, logic, or language would be illusory.

If *laws of logic* emanate from the *physical* body, and are the result of "mere chance...then it necessarily follows that the molecules of the human brain are also the product of mere chance. In other words, we think the way we do simply because the atoms and molecules of our brain happen to have combined in the way they have, totally without transcendent guidance or control. So then even the philosophies of men, their systems of logic, and all their approaches to reality are the result of mere fortuity."[80]

This is certainly not how most people, including philosophers, conceive logic. Laws of logic are "certainly not reducible to matter since if they were they would not be laws – laws are not something that can be physically examined. Moreover, since the principles of logic are universal in nature they are not reducible to any particular physical object or objects. But if they are not reducible matter what are they? It does no good to say they are mental abstractions since neither abstractions nor minds are possible within an atheist worldview. Nor can they be conventional since if they were they could be changed. And if they can be changed then absurdities follow – the statement that Bill Clinton is President of the United States could be both true and false."[81]

The problem of explaining laws of logic in a materialistic universe has led a number of anti-theists to try and account for them by saying that logic, whatever it is, is simply inescapable, because in order to try and deny human reason it must first be exercised. In other words, logic stands by itself, on the basis of man's experience. In order to be consistent with this answer though, the one holding this opinion would have to be open to the possibility that the laws of logic could be *disproved* by finite human experience in the future. Anti-theists often ignore the point that just because logic is inescapable does not mean it is without *preconditions*.

Anti-theism must offer some kind of metaphysical foundation for the universality of logic. Logic reflects coherent thinking. And coherent thinking takes place within a mind. One may ask *whose mind* sets the *universal* standard for man's logical thought? Laws of logic are not floating around somewhere in the cosmos. If cognitive abilities originate within the movement of mindless atoms then atheism should also posit a rational response to the question, "How is it possible to start with randomness and arrive at intelligence?"

Although many anti-theists are quick to accuse theists of taking positions they regard as irrational, they are conversely unwilling to admit that their presuppositions about reality render the concept of reason itself meaningless. "Naturalistic theories teach in effect that the human mind is the chance by-product of an irrational and mindless process. This means that carried to its logical conclusion, the natural evolutionary theory strips away the basis for rationality itself. It reduces human reason to biochemical and electrical mechanisms. Those who argue that man's thoughts can be fully explained as the result of irrational causes are in reasoning attempting to prove that there are no such things as proofs. It is a self-defeating process to use human reason to call into question the validity of human reason."[82]

The source of human personality is also unexplainable apart from the Bible's depiction of the transcendent nature of self-consciousness. The atheist should explain how *personality* could rise out of an *impersonal* universe. Materialistic atheism cannot "explain the personality of man. Personality (including intellect, emotion, and will) is on a higher order than impersonality, and yet the naturalist maintains that this is a product of impersonal chance factors. However...no effect can be greater than its cause. Personality cannot be derived from an entirely impersonal basis."[83]

Beginning with an impersonal universe wherein man is a mere product of nature has even led some to conclude that human beings have no more intrinsic worth than any other creature. What makes a person's life of greater value than the life of any other evolved "animal"? In the words of one animal rights activist, "Animal liberationists do not separate out the human animal, so there is no basis for saying that a human being has special rights. A rat is a pig is a dog is a boy. They're all mammals."[84] Man is just one more beast among many to arrive on the scene through chance causes.

Non theistic views also strip life of objective meaning. Meaningful existence is directly dependent upon whether or not our lives have *purpose*. But where does man derive the purpose of his existence? It cannot arise out of a purely natural environment because unsupervised and undirected random matter does not have objective purpose; it merely "is". Since man's life in an atheistic universe would be the result of blind natural processes then objective meaning cannot be derived, or even assumed, from within such a universe.

Objective meaning cannot be generated from within one's own finite existence. Meaning cannot originate from within our own individual world of personal relationships, economic pursuits, benevolent work or altruistic expressions because there is always a "bigger picture" with which we must reference them. "Activity does not create meaning; it is the other way around. If life in its existential expression has no meaning, then a change of attitude does not change the reality of meaninglessness...Life is punctuated with tiny little purposes and no ultimate purpose: tiny little values, but no ultimate value."[85] In order to have genuine meaning life must be placed within some kind of philosophical framework from which it can derive a meaningful purpose. Meaning must be defined by *referencing something greater than the individual.* But if the human condition is ultimately just a result of "atoms banging around"[86] then attaching significance to our own mortal existence is self-delusion against the reality of nihilism.[87]

Biblical Christianity begins with God's revelation instead of nature. Genesis teaches us that man is not the offspring of nature, but rather a special creature. In contrast to other creatures only man bears the image of God. Man reflects some of the attributes of his Creator. Man's nature is comprised of body and soul. This soul possesses self-consciousness, intellect, will, and moral conscience. These immaterial characteristics of the soul metaphysically account for the possibility of abstract free thought and self-awareness. God's attributes reflected within the immaterial part of man's nature reflect the meaning of man's existence and enable him to have knowledge of it.

Christianity accounts for human personality because in the Christian worldview there is no impersonal universe. Man is not an impersonal entity. Human beings are unique, *personal* beings. But personality did not just appear out of nothingness. Personality existed prior to man because there was a personal God from whom man has derived personal characteristics.

This same God provides a purpose for life. Our existence, relationships, emotions, work and even painful circumstances are all meaningful experiences set within the context of knowing that God has a divine plan for mankind that is being progressively accomplished through time. Our life, and its accomplishments, does not end in physical death. Death in the Bible is never portrayed as cessation but rather a transition of life. The Christian's purposeful existence is not impeded by physical death. The eternal life God offers transcends material barriers. Our individual existence has meaning because it is woven into the fabric of God's eternal plan.

As creatures created in God's image, man possesses a mind that is able to truly think and reason, although on a finite scale. "...God's thinking represents perfect coherence. Therefore, in order for men to know things...they too must think coherently or with logical consistency...the Christian views logic as a reflection of God's own thinking, rather than as laws or principles that are 'higher' than God or that exist 'in independence of God and man.'"[88] "The Christian finds, further, that logic agrees with the [biblical] story. Human logic agrees with the story, *because it derives its meaning from the story.*"[89]

For any interpretation of creation to be coherent or logical it must be interpreted within the boundaries of God's revelation. Thus "we engage in conceptual reasoning (utilizing universals and laws) because we have been created in God's image and thus can think His thoughts after Him on the finite, creaturely level."[90]

Scripture allows for finite man to have an assurance of true knowledge about the infinite cosmos without actually possessing infinite knowledge himself. In Christian theology it is God who has knowledge of all things. Every aspect of reality has been conceived by God, conditioned by God and is presently known by God. When man comes to "know" any fact or truth he is discovering a portion of that which God exhaustively knows. Man's knowledge is grounded in the sure foundational truths that God reveals in His Word. We can be confident that sure knowledge is possible even if we ourselves aren't in possession of infinite knowledge because the epistemological basis for our knowledge is secure.

Man's knowledge of anything, especially himself, begins with his knowledge of God. "God made man a rational-moral creature. He will always be that. As such he is confronted with God...To not know God man would have to destroy himself..."[91] With atheistic presuppositions it is impossible to rationally interpret human nature, personality or experience, but within Christianity they have a firm metaphysical basis.

10
Creation or Evolution?

When Charles Darwin published the *Origin of the Species* in 1859 he offered an explanation for life's origins completely opposite to that of the Bible's creation story. The book of Genesis says, "In the beginning God created", but Darwin's view assumes the personal creator revealed in scripture isn't the necessary first cause for all life.

The Bible roots the beginning of the cosmos in the supernatural, but Darwinism is rooted in naturalism. Christianity regards man to be a special creature who was created by God for His special purposes. Evolution teaches that man is one of many evolved animals. Scripture speaks of God making all things for His glory, sustaining all things by His power, and providing meaning to all things in the cosmos. Darwin's theory asserts that every living thing is the result of random forces within a completely natural evolutionary process. Darwinism conceives of the universe as a closed system operating on its own apart from any divine control.

The Bible's theology is not opposed to the fact that there are continuously occurring variations *within* reproductive communities. What it does clearly teach is that existing species do not mutate into new interbreeding species. Biblical Christianity opposes Darwinian evolution, also known as macro-evolutionary theory. According to Genesis all living creatures produce "after their kind" in accordance with God's design. (Genesis 1:21) Documenting changes that occur *within* species is not the same as offering proof that chance causes resulting from natural selection have created *brand new* species. This distinction is extremely important because the term "evolution" is applied to both concepts and many arguments substitute examples of the former in order to prove the latter.

The debate over Darwinian evolution has intensified in recent years largely as a result of some highly publicized works from a number of scientists who, although not creationists, are still very critical of macro-evolutionary theory. Creationists, however, have consistently pointed out over the years that the vast amount of biological, archeological and chemical data available from research does not and never did support Darwin's theory.

It is certainly true that creationists take their faith into account when they evaluate scientific data and they are certainly motivated by their religious convictions. But the fact is evolutionists also maintain their basic claims on an enduring *faith* that eons of time must have eventually produced what cannot be duplicated through observed natural selection. When evolutionists boldly assert statements such as, "Man is the result of a purposeless and natural process that did not have him in mind"92, they should also admit that they are not operating within the boundaries of mere scientific observation.

Naturalistic Darwinism appears to be the accepted *metaphysical paradigm* of the majority of scientists. Evolution never has to be *proven* to them. It is assumed to be correct while creationism is generally never taken very seriously. But this does not prove macroevolution is true. Just because it is possible to *imagine* such evolution might have taken place does not mean it did. History provides many recorded instances where theories once considered scientifically orthodox have been discarded.

Macro-evolutionary dogma is so dominant within the scientific and academic establishment that even many Christians have felt constrained to embrace some of its propositions in order to maintain an appearance of intellectual credibility. They do this while also trying to somehow work "God" into its framework.

Their resulting "theistic evolution" is a vain attempt to merge the theory of evolution with the personal creator revealed in scripture.

Self-proclaimed theistic evolutionists have a biblical dilemma. Since the theory of evolution and the Bible posit opposite anthropological and historical truth-claims, these theists have tried to resolve their logical tension by metaphorically reinterpreting Genesis. Then they try to explain how both the Bible and evolutionary theory are basically correct. Evolution has taken place, say the theists, but it is God who directed the process.

These are well-intentioned efforts to defend the integrity of the Bible; however, interpreting the book of Genesis as something other than an actual historical record creates many more interpretive problems for Bible readers than it would first appear to resolve. "Absolutely every place where the New Testament refers to the first half of Genesis, the New Testament assumes (and many times affirms) that Genesis is history, and that it is to be read in normal fashion with the common use of the words and syntax."[93] This is obviously true throughout the Old Testament as well.

Christians often fail to understand that making concessions to any aspect of evolutionary theory automatically infers that the Bible is less than completely credible as an authoritative source for religious truth. Every major doctrine of orthodox biblical Christianity has its roots in Genesis. Christian theology and history merge in the pages of scripture. The Bible records God's works in human history. These works are important facts contained within Christian theology. Altering any aspect of what the Bible records as history undermines every doctrine in Christian theology. If the book of Genesis is not the historical account it's portrayed to be then the whole Christian belief system falls apart.

The book of Genesis is written as an historical narrative. It states life on earth came into being through a six-day supernatural creation by the hand of God. If this claim were not true then it would be easy to understand why most scientists should be skeptical regarding truth-claims associated with Christian theology. If the Bible's factual claims regarding cosmology are in error then why should anybody seriously consider what it teaches about sin? In Christianity, the history of sin entering into humanity is derived from the book of Genesis. If the Bible's historical claims are false then people are justified in doubting the contents of its theology also. Many non-Christians correctly recognize that if events recorded as history in the Bible could be proven false then its central message can also be called into question.

Darwinian evolutionists usually tolerate religious beliefs only if they are kept strictly compartmentalized from science. One prominent evolutionist writes, "No scientific theory, including evolution, can pose any threat to religion – for these two great tools of human understanding operate in complementary (not contrary) fashion in their totally separate realms: science as an inquiry about the factual state of the natural world, religion as a search for spiritual meaning and ethical values."[94] Here the author states that only science is qualified to be an authority on "the factual state of the natural world." Does that mean religion can't speak about such facts? To an evolutionist the discovery of *facts* must come from science, not religion. But if this were true then religion's only duty would be to make so-called value judgements based upon such facts. Science, not religion, is the clearly superior discipline in this case.

Although the writer claims science and religion hold equal positions, his statement implies that science has now supplanted theology as the primary discipline from which one can make ultimate or factual truth-claims. This is why many of the "very same persons who insist upon keeping religion and science separate are eager to use their science as a basis for pronouncements about religion. The literature of Darwinism is full of anti-theistic conclusions such as the universe was not designed and has no purpose, and that we humans are the product of blind natural processes that care nothing about us."[95]

How can a religion provide individuals with "spiritual meaning" if its metaphysical contentions regarding the natural world are false? It is impossible to separate Christianity's *spiritual truths* from its *factual assertions* about the natural world because its metaphysic interweaves them together. This is true of *every* other religion as well.

If the cosmos exists because of natural evolutionary forces then such a truth would carry implications with it. Religious beliefs and the "ethical values" associated with them could never be considered equal to facts about the natural world. Anyone's ethical opinions would be just as good (or worthless) as another's because they are arbitrary. This assumes that one could actually make sense of such facts apart from the Christian worldview, which they cannot. But the point here is that ethical relativism is one of the unavoidable implications of Darwinism.

One does not have to study Darwinism for long to realize that it isn't as much science as it is a *philosophy of science.* Darwin's theory is philosophically constructed upon the foundation of naturalism. Naturalism is the belief that "nature" is the only reality that provably exists. The terms *naturalism* and *materialism* refer to the same metaphysical outlook in this book because naturalists assume that "nature" basically consists of the particles found in matter and energy.

Modern science is identified with naturalism itself, which serves to automatically define creationism as something other than "science." "The scientist who believes in naturalism is biased in favor of Darwinism even before he examines the evidence."[96] Charles Darwin believed in a science "committed to thoroughly naturalistic explanations based on material causes and the uniformity of nature".[97]

> The most common objection to any notion of design is that it falls outside the range of science – that any theory involving reference to an intelligent agent is

unscientific. But this objection assumes a particular definition of science...In fact, many philosophers of science now recognize that proposed principles of demarcation are themselves philosophically charged - that they reflect the metaphysical presuppositions of the person proposing them...the principles offered for defining science really function as weapons in philosophical battles.[98]

Simply put, those who believe in macroevolution will argue it must have happened because their own naturalistic worldview will not *permit* any other explanation for life's origin. Darwinists use naturalistic assumptions to interpret all scientific data in such a way as to prove their theory. Among these assumptions:

a) It is not possible to truly know if something exists outside of the material universe.

b) Everything in existence is the result of "natural" causes.

c) It is not the job of science to speculate upon the possibility of supra-natural causes because such metaphysical considerations are out of the realm of scientific inquiry.

These mistaken assumptions reveal naturalism's (and evolution's) flaws. The first error naturalists make is the assumption that if something transcends the physical world it cannot be known. Naturalists generally maintain that it is impossible to truly know if *metaphysical* realities exist because they cannot be empirically verified. But this overlooks the fact that this assertion is itself a *metaphysical* claim. The *belief* that something cannot be known unless it is measured against some type of empirical standard is itself a metaphysical judgement that cannot be empirically demonstrated.

Secondly, a consistent adherence to naturalism would actually undermine all scientific study. Scientific investigation requires metaphysical commitments to unseen laws, logic, theory and methodology. While science has always concerned itself with the underlying natural causes that affect the physical world the controlling forces behind matter and energy and the tools of reason used to inquire about them are *immaterial*. These realities are clearly not material in nature and cannot be accounted for in a naturalistic worldview. If naturalists fully adhered to their worldview they would have to forgo all scientific reasoning and speculation.

In addition, the mechanics of the universe can only be understood if we are allowed to assume that the future will be like present and past experiences. This belief is essential to inductive reasoning, which is applied in scientific experimentation. A naturalistic worldview provides no guarantee that the future will be like the past because without belief in a sovereign God who governs the universe and maintains its uniformity the world is left to *chance*. Yet chance occurrences do not provide any basis for *uniformity* in nature.

It is impossible for anyone, including naturalists, to be free of metaphysical commitments in their reasoning. Since naturalism can only be defended through *metaphysical* claims it refutes itself. Metaphysical beliefs are always present in science. The truth is that both biblical creationism and Darwinian evolution are faith-views. Both of them contain certain metaphysical assumptions.

The presuppositions of Darwin's naturalism and supernatural creationism are in vivid contrast to one another. Since the basic assumption held by naturalists is that only natural things exist, they refuse to even recognize the *possibility* of supernatural realities like those found in the Bible. This is why naturalists often ask Christians rhetorical questions like, "If God made the universe then who made God?" or "How could God have made the universe out of nothing?" But evolution's proponents are challenged with similar questions. According to their worldview the evolutionist must either presuppose that the material universe came out of nothing or that matter is eternal. This reveals a double standard because evolutionists cannot correspondingly provide answers as to *how* something can come from nothing or *how* it is possible for matter to simply pre-exist apart from a natural cause.

In the Christian worldview, God's Being transcends the cosmos. His eternal Being, *by definition*, is timeless and spaceless. He is not subject to the natural limitations or conditions of the realm that He both created and now oversees. Using these assumptions it is not necessary to comprehend *how* God transcends the cosmos. What becomes necessary to acknowledge is that His being is a rationally required precondition for its existence. While it would *not be possible* for the natural cosmos to exist without a natural cause (i.e. create itself out of nothing), it would be *possible* for an omnipotent Creator to use means wholly inaccessible or unexplainable to finite man to create the cosmos out of nothing. This isn't a comprehensive answer, but it is a *rational* one *if* one first presupposes God's attributes as revealed in the Bible. If the God of the Bible is presupposed then a supernatural six-day creation is certainly metaphysically possible.

A naturalistic worldview also assumes that there are causal factors in the universe, which can be described in law-like principles. Nature supposedly has "laws" within it that somehow determine the behavior of matter and energy. While even many Christians often support this view of natural law theory it is theologically heterodox. There is no basis for a "semi-autonomous, self-operating realm of 'nature' whose impersonal laws are occasionally 'violated' by the God who reveals Himself in scripture."[99] Such thinking reflects Deism, not orthodox Christianity.[100] "In fact, the Bible offers us a view of the world which is quite contrary to this, one where God and His agents are seen as intimately, continuously, and directly involved in all of the detailed events which transpire in the created order." (Isaiah 40:7,

59:19, 63:14; Psalm 104:29-30; Proverbs 16:33; Matthew 10:30)
101

Science is provided with a sure metaphysical basis for regularities in nature by presupposing that God providentially governs the universe. But if naturalism is presupposed then there is a huge philosophical problem. On the one hand, naturalists must affirm that nature keeps *itself* uniform. Since no outside governing force over the universe can be known (supernatural or otherwise) naturalists must assume the universe governs itself. On the other hand they must also affirm that nature *violates* the very laws producing its regularities in order to create the macro-changes necessary for evolution to take place.

Naturalists are forced to affirm two contradictory presuppositions. Naturalism provides no answer as to how the very laws producing *uniformity in* nature also lend themselves over to the *evolution of* nature? If naturalists state that nature violates its own laws in order to account for macroevolution they are essentially allowing for interruptions in the normal and predictable operations of nature while simultaneously refusing to make allowances for miraculous works of God within the same realm.

It is evident that interpretation of so-called facts is controlled by whatever paradigm we are willing to accept by faith. Naturalists, like Christians, have distinct faith commitments. Naturalistic assumptions preclude supernatural attributes of God to be at work in creation. But they will allow for some of these very same attributes to reside within nature.

Naturalists consider nature to be *sovereign* in the sense that there is no acknowledged superior metaphysical existence. They believe nature is *self-sufficient* in that it does not depend upon anything outside of itself. They also essentially believe that *miracles* occur in nature in that there must be interruptions in the way nature normally works for macroevolution to take place. A nature-only worldview replaces belief in the supernatural personal

God of scripture with an impersonal mystical deity often simply referred to as "nature". The faith-assumptions of the naturalist, although self-undermining, are still the preferred *religious assumptions* of modern science.

11

Thoughts on World Religion

A short, single chapter such as this can do little more than begin the task of offering a critique of the many religious views expressed throughout the world. It must be noted from the outset that religious views held by millions of people are certainly worthy of much more discussion than what will be found here.

Although practical limitations prevent a study of every major world religion even a concise defense of the Christian worldview necessitates some comments regarding world religions. "It is the Christian's contention that all non-Christian worldviews are beset with internal contradictions, as well as with beliefs which do not render logic, science, or ethics intelligible."[102] This brief examination is offered as a vehicle to stimulate further inquiry into the problems characteristically found within non-Christian religious views.

One repeatedly stressed point within this book has been that *all* belief systems, whether secular or religious, are really faith-based systems. Every worldview has its own set of peculiar presuppositions its proponents will hold to in faith. Faith lies at the heart of every worldview. But religious belief systems are generally regarded as holding to some sort of spiritual or transcendent dimension to reality. Different religions, however, widely vary in their conception of that reality. There are almost an infinite variety of religious claims made, for example, about who or what is "GOD."

In today's cultural climate it is often considered offensive for anyone to assert that their religion's doctrines are true while others' are not. Many simply take it for granted that because metaphysical affirmations are found in all religions, no particular sect of religious believers can ever really claim that their beliefs are objectively true. Religious beliefs are simply regarded as subjective preferences that exist apart from objective facts. Thus, all religions are looked upon as sincere expressions of people's faith.

Mahatma Gandhi, arguably the most famous 20th century Hindu, said that he hoped everyone "may develop to the fullness of his being in his own religion - that the Christian may become a better Christian and the Mohammedan a better Mohammedan."[103] The well-known Hindu philosopher Ramakrishna similarly echoed, "So people in ignorance say, 'My religion is the only one, my religion is best.' But when a heart is illumined by true knowledge, it knows that above all these wars of sects and sectarians preside the one indivisible eternal, all-knowing bliss."[104]

Untold numbers of people voice similar thoughts when they suggest that all religions are merely different roads leading to the same heaven. But while such sentiments may convey a legitimate desire not to be narrow-minded or offensive to others they really do not even begin to address the underlying question as to how systematic religious truth-claims so different from each other can all simultaneously be true.

Pluralists often try to superficially blend together certain religious doctrines to make it appear that the world's major religions essentially teach the same basic truths. What they fail to note, however, is that although religions may contain elements reflecting similar characteristics, their constructs are not the same. When it comes to belief systems the details are just as important as the generalities.

Despite what others may insist, world religions do not teach the same things. The Buddha (enlightened one) offered his teachings, in contrast to Hinduism, as a true representation of the way to personal salvation. Gandhi, on the other hand, wrote in his

Autobiography that, "truth is the sovereign principle, and the *Bhagavad-Gita* is the book *par excellence* for the knowledge of Truth."[105] Leaders of Hinduism, Buddhism, Islam and other religions, like adherents to any belief system, promote certain religious ideas with the apparent conviction that they reflect reality. "Anyone who claims that all religions are the same betrays not only an ignorance of all religions but also a caricatured view of even the best-known ones. Every religion at its core is exclusive."[106]

Religious beliefs are supposed to offer profound answers to life's most fundamental questions. Such answers are only possible if a religion gives human beings a description of reality as it actually is. Religious worldviews are comprised of systematic truth-claims. The notion of truth is implied in every religion's teaching.

Truth-claims associated with particular worldviews are either true or they are not. This makes it all the more important that such beliefs be truth-tested. "A true defense of any claim must also deal with the evidences that challenge or contradict it. In other words, truth is not only a matter of offense, in that it makes certain assertions. It is also a matter of defense, in that it must be able to make a cogent and sensible response to the counterpoints that are raised."[107]

The fact that religious beliefs are filled with truth-claims underscores why reason can never be separated from them. While finite human logic is not to be taken as supreme, blind faith goes to the opposite extreme. Religious beliefs should never be insulated from reason. This does not mean, of course, that limitations upon man's ability to understand *everything* about reality should be confused with irrationalism. It is one thing for someone to admit that as finite creatures we cannot possess unlimited comprehension of the nature of reality, but it is another thing entirely to try and affirm truth-claims that fundamentally undermine each other.

The Bible indicates that non-Christian views always harbor internal and unresolvable systematic tensions. Philosophical inconsistencies always reside in the heart of unscriptural belief systems. A brief survey of Hinduism's main doctrines may serve as an example for this chapter.

Hinduism contains a fundamental belief referred to as *monism*. This is a conviction that everything in reality is made up of the same substance, whether that substance is matter, mind, or something else. Hinduism portrays ultimate reality as one, all encompassing, unified, world soul. "The name the Hindus give to supreme reality is *Brahman*...utter reality, utter consciousness, and utterly beyond all possibility of frustration – this is the basic Hindu view of God."[108] Much of the music and writing within popular culture, such as the lyrics in the famous Beatles song, *I am the Walrus*, reflect monism. "I am he as you are he as you are me and we are all together..." Monism essentially means *all is one*.

An objective definition of *Brahman* outside of vague descriptions of "oneness" really is not possible. "On the whole India has been content to encourage the devotee to conceive of *Brahman* as either personal or transpersonal, depending, on which carries the most exalted meaning for the mind in question."[109] The basic composition of this supposed ultimate reality is left up to an adherent's subjective opinion.

Describing *Brahman* itself presents this concept's first logical challenge. Contending that reality is "oneness" first requires a person to ignore the fact that reality appears to contain distinctions. There is a sharp contrast here between Hindu doctrine and human experience. Human beings must operate as if real differences exist in the world. After all, isn't there a *difference* between Hinduism and other religions? The Hindu is declaring a unique (i.e. different) faith while theoretically positing everything in fact is one (i.e. the same).

The Hindu response to this is that even though reality appears to contain distinctions, this appearance is really just *maya*, which means illusion. While this answer is in accord with the concept of monism it also undermines an individual's assurance of its truth. If "all is one" then apparent distinctions between both physical and mental states are illusory also. This calls into question not only one's perceptions about any religious knowledge but every other aspect of human experience as well. It is not practical "to live day after day in a world where chairs seem real and your mother seems real and love seems real and to keep insisting they're just *maya*."[110]

The Hindu's ultimate goal is for the individual's soul (*atman*) to be ultimately united with the one encompassing world-soul or *Brahman*. This journey supposedly takes place throughout the course of many re-incarnations, or re-births upon the wheel of life. Hinduism teaches that the cosmic law of *karma* pre-determines one's status in the present life while also determining their future birth-status in the next one. "The literal meaning of *karma* (as we encountered it in the *karma yoga*) is work, but as a doctrine it means, roughly, the moral law of cause and effect...The present condition of each interior life - how happy it is, how confused or serene, how much it sees - is an exact product of what it has wanted and done in the past."[111]

The ideas of reincarnation and karma were once strongly tied to the ancient Indian caste system, with its rigid lines of distinction between the various social classes. Strict adherence to caste rules was believed to bring a reward of rebirth into a higher caste in the future life. "Caste rules preventing a Hindu from eating, marrying, and all intimate dealings with persons who belong to the other main casts, were even to the other subcasts of his own main caste, though it should be said that the 20th-century has witnessed a progressive breakdown of caste in India."[112] Indians once looked upon re-incarnation as the primary vehicle for social advancement.

Hindu scriptures teach that karma brings punishment also. "Hindu folklore abounds in legends about the workings of karma.

In one group of morality tales, for example a foolish man is reborn a monkey, a cunning one as a jackal, a greedy one as a crow. A tribal myth of Orissa tells of a woman burning with jealousy who is reborn as a chili plant, destined to burn all its life. Conversely, an animal may rise to human status, in stages or all at once if it has done the right deeds, particularly to a personage of high caste."[113]

Hinduism teaches that human beings may be reborn as animal, vegetable, or even mineral substances. "Those whose conduct has been good, will quickly attain some good birth, the birth of a Brahmana (*priestly class*), or a Kshatriya (*warrior class*), or a Vaisya (*professional class*). But those whose conduct has been evil, will quickly attain an evil birth, the birth of a dog, or a hog, or a Kandala (*outcast*). (my italics) [114]

The full Hindu view of re-incarnation is typically more than the average western mind wants to digest, which is why non-easterners usually only borrow selective elements from it to incorporate into their worldview. One such element is the notion that some type of moral law governs human actions. The doctrine of karma is Hinduism's answer as to why man should be a "moral" being who takes responsibility for his actions.

The belief in karma, however, brings with it more than just a notion that man lives within a moral universe. If karma is real then individuals inevitably face a predetermined fate in this life that cannot be altered. Human conditions are already bound and determined by choices made in a previous life. With this kind of determinism though, the conditions of the *previous* life would be representative of the life lived *before* that one, and so on, into the past. If this is true then isn't it legitimate to ask just how much actual freedom or personal responsibility one currently exercises regarding the choices or state of their present life?

In addition, the doctrine of karma was strongly integrated with the former caste system. Since that ancient class structure has now been officially banned in India the rules once supposed to be the standard by which men's actions were measured have been removed. What moral standard is now applied by the workings of karma to determine either blessings or curses?

In studying karma it is also unclear what exactly the relationship was between the presupposed law of karma and the ancient rules of caste? If the formerly imposed rules of caste determined how karma would judge men, then this means finite man had the power to create the supposedly higher cosmic laws that judged him. But if the ancient rules of caste were derived from the higher law of karma then Hinduism is now disregarding the rules that karma continues to apply when judging man. Its standard is now unattainable since the cast system has officially been eradicated.

Perhaps the greatest internal moral contradiction within Hinduism is that its doctrine of Brahman implies that all circumstances, including those resulting from direct human actions, are ultimately an expression of that same reality. While karma recognizes "good" behavior such as altruism and unselfishness, the concept of Brahman itself reduces all human actions to moral equivalence. Philosophically speaking, Hinduism actually eliminates the distinction between good and evil. If all is one, then *good and evil are one* also.

Hindu philosophers may counter by saying that only an individual's ultimate unity with Brahman could permit them to transcend all ethical distinctions. But the fact is that if Brahman is a true picture of reality then all of the laws man lives by on this earth implying right from wrong, or good versus evil, are really out of synch with reality itself. "Such a one, verily, the thought does not torment: 'Why have I not done the good?' 'Why have I done the evil?' He who knows this, saves himself from both these thoughts. For truly, from both of these he saves himself - he who knows this. This is the Upanishad mystic doctrine."[115]

One final thought on this point is that Orthodox Hinduism's doctrine of karma essentially implies an impersonal universe. Since karma itself is seen judging man's actions there is no place for any personal judge. It leads one to wonder how karma, with its ability to distinguish "right" from "wrong" behavior in a universe where all is "one" came into being in the first place? And how can there be moral law without a *moral lawgiver*?

Notions of a moral lawgiver usually lead one back to the subject of God. What exactly does Hinduism teach about *God*? Though Hinduism teaches the idea of an impersonal *Brahman* as true reality it also attempts to accommodate every pagan notion of deity as well. "Idolatry is abundantly manifest throughout Hindu India. It is directed toward all kinds of human and animal representations, and even to images of the male and female sexual organs."[116]

A Hindu may be atheistic in the sense that they believe Brahman or ultimate reality consists of some sort of impersonal substance. Hindu scriptures, on the other hand, such as the Bhagavad Gita and Bhagavata Purana attribute authoritative statements to personal gods in their literature. This may be why it appears the "average man in India is polytheistic, because he reveres all supernatural beings; and of these there is no end. To the Hindu his deities number, as he often says, 330,000,000 gods."[117]

Hindu teachers constantly mix the language of personality with impersonality in their efforts to explain what *Brahman* means. "As one and the same material, water, is called by different names by different peoples, one calling it *water*, another *eau*, a third *aqua*, and another *pani*, so the one Everlasting-Intelligent-Bliss is invoked by some as *God*, by some as *Allah*, by some as *Jehovah*, and by others as *Brahman*."[118]

Attempting to find a straightforward answer to the question of whether or not a supreme personal being exists is not possible within Hinduism. As one leading Hindu Philosopher said, "Those who live in God do not care to define. They have a particular confidence in the universe, a profound and peaceful acceptance of life in all its sides. Their response to Ultimate Reality is not capable of a clear cut, easily intelligible formulation. The mystery of God's being cannot be rationally determined. It remains outside the scope of logical concepts."[119]

How can the Hindu philosopher *know* that God's being falls outside the scope of logical concepts? Would not his use of logic in this statement imply that logic itself must be an expression of ultimate reality? If so, then how is it that logic cannot somehow correspond with human descriptions about God? What the Hindu is admitting, of course, is that *Hinduism's* concept of God falls completely outside of logic. This is the heart of this negative internal critique of Hinduism as a worldview. Hindu descriptions of God always end up as irrational, contradictory or unintelligible abstract formulations. By trying to accommodate every possible definition of God, Hinduism strips real meaning from any of them.

If monism (all is one) is true, then one could easily conclude that pantheism (all is god) is also true. Man himself can be considered a god. It is not surprising that this is exactly what one finds in many writings of those influenced by Hindu thought. "This is the heart of philosophical Hinduism – self-deification. One of India's premier philosophers stated as forthrightly as one could, "Man is God in a temporary state of self-forgetfulness."[120] The desire to be like God, with the power to decide right from wrong, is exactly what the Bible says led Adam and Eve to their downfall.

Hinduism seems to emphasize either one of two extremes. While monistic doctrine leads certain Hindus to think that man himself is god, Hindu scripture often leads others into primitive paganism. But worshiping a plurality of deities introduces its own problems from a rational standpoint. "The word *gods* itself is problematic. The very word God implies and requires sovereignty. This is why the word *gods* implies a contradiction: because the so-called gods imply by that title sovereignty, which they do not possess; they can only be seen as partially gods, i.e., one god controlled sea voyages; another, sexual matters; still another, warfare and so on. Polytheism has many partially ruling spirits, but no God."[121]

The Bible teaches that only faith and obedience to the Being who has revealed Himself through His Word lead to genuine worship of God. It teaches that the world's religions, and their practices, are just the false creations of men. The main issue for people should not be whether or not this message offends them, but whether or not the Bible is accurate about its portrayal of the one true God who wants no false gods before Him. (Ex 20:1-6)

Conclusion

Everyone is committed to some kind of faith. Each one of us has a worldview. No worldview is neutral. There are faith-assumptions, or presuppositions at the base of each that we use to interpret all of reality. This is the heart of the matter when speaking of having a "right" as opposed to a "wrong" philosophy of life. Even so, these faith commitments go far beyond mere intellectual commitment. They touch the very core of our being. They are part of our spiritual and moral essence. Each of us has motives for holding to the particular view of reality we use to define our lives. God tries our hearts and knows these motives. (Ps 66:10)

The evidence for the existence of the God of the Bible is abundantly demonstrated in His Word, His creation and the creaturehood of man. The key to Christian conversion does not hinge upon the need for more evidence, but rather a change of heart. This change permits us to have the "eyes to see and ears to hear" God's revelation of Himself. (Mk 8:17-18; Acts 13:48)

God is not interested in anyone merely giving mental assent to his existence. God is after something much more. Truly knowing God "is rather part of a process of God's thorough make-over of a person. It is, from our human standpoint, an active commitment to a morally transforming personal relationship. We come to know God only as God becomes our God, the Lord of our lives...God refuses, for our own good, to become a mere idol of our thought or entertainment."[122]

There are those who say that if they could personally witness some sort of miraculous sign they would then be brought into a position where they could believe the Bible. Yet the Bible teaches that even when Christ performed many miracles in the midst of the crowds most people did not believe he was God. "Miraculous events do not impose their interpretation on us. We interpreters must decide on our interpretations of events, and various background beliefs and motives typically influence our interpretive decisions. We thus should not regard miraculous signs as effective *for all inquirers*."[123] Most of the people who followed Jesus' earthly ministry in the gospels were seeking a show, not spiritual renewal.

It is highly unlikely that most people who become Christians embrace the Christian faith because they have systematically reasoned about its doctrines in contrast to the beliefs held by other worldviews. One thing, however, is sure. No one can ever truly come to Christ without first presupposing His Word.

An individual's confession of Jesus Christ as personal Lord and Savior (Rom 10:9-13) only comes with the presupposition that both His person and Work are truly what the Bible reveals them to be. This is why orthodox Christian theology is so important. As one Christian apologist put it, "...if you do not listen to Theology, that will not mean that you have no ideas about God. It will mean that you have a lot of wrong ones – bad, muddled, out-of-date ideas."[124] Have our notions about God come from human imagination or His revelation?

God created man as a finite creature. Man was created to be dependent upon God and His revelation. Man's fall into sin was essentially a rejection of this dependence. "This, then, is the essence of sin; man's rebellion against recognizing his dependence on God in everything and the assumption of his ability to be *independent* of God."[125] The serpent's temptation in Genesis was for man to be "like God". It still is. Whether man uses his presupposed independence to deny God's existence or reinterpret God's truth in world religion, man's absolute dependence upon God still remains. Reality is what scripture reveals it to be.

Conclusion

It is only in Scripture that man may rightly comprehend God as He really is (holy Creator), and at the same time comprehend himself as he really is (sinful creature). All men have a belief in God (even those who do not acknowledge such belief), yet this is not the same as saving knowledge...the only way God can properly be known (savingly) is by the prior submission to God which results in true devotion and piety. It is impossible for man the creature to escape the knowledge of God as his Creator/judge.[126]

By presupposing the Bible as God's Word and yielding control of their life to Christ, their creator, individuals come full circle. They move from supposed independence and self-sufficiency to acknowledged dependence upon their creator, just as Adam did before the Fall. This dependence is the way God always intended it should be. We must hold fast to "the Christian worldview if we are to make sense of argumentation about, reasoning about, and interpretation of, any element of human experience. Without the assumption of Christian theism, there would be no basis for believing that there is order, connection, predictability, or necessity anywhere in human experience."[127] True knowledge and understanding of life begins with His Word.

ENDNOTES

1 Phillip R. Johnson, "The Law of Contradiction", in Grace To You, par. 1 [online ministry] (1995 [cited 1 May 2002]) ; available from World Wide Web at http://www.gty.org/~phil/articles/lawofcon.htm.

2 Gary, DeMar, "Living With Contradictions," *Biblical Worldview* (February 2000), p. 3.

3 Paul Copan, *"True For You, But Not For Me"* (Minneapolis, MN: Bethany House Publishers, 1998), p. 35.

4 Thomas Nagel, quoted by Ravi Zacharias, "Lessons From War In A Battle Of Ideas," *Just thinking* (Fall 2000: RZIM) pp. 4-5.

5 Ravi Zacharias, *Jesus Among Other Gods* (Word Publishing, Nashville, TN, 2000), p.48.

6 Christian philosopher Francis Schaeffer often referred to *reality* using these terms collectively. See Francis A. Schaeffer, *Trilogy* (Westchester, Ill: Crossway Books, 1990), p.263.

7 *Reality* as it is used here refers to everything that truly exists, whether natural, supra-natural, material, immaterial, personal, conscious or spiritual.

8 J.I. Packer and Thomas Howard, "Meet Secular Humanism," in *Salt and Light*, ed. David J. Gyertson (Dallas, TX: Word Publishing, 1993), pp. 75-76.

9 George Grant, "What? The Purpose of the Lives", *Stirling Bridge* (September 1997, King's Meadow Study Center), p. 3.

10 Greg Bahnsen, *Always Ready* (Texarkana, AK: Covenant Media Foundation, 1996), p. 216.

11 Cornelius Van Til quoted in Greg Bahnsen, "Package Deals," *Penpoint* (Placentia, CA: Southern California Study Center For Christian Studies, Vol. 6, No. 7, 1995), p. 1.

12 To be "secular" is to live one's life with an orientation towards the present world, as opposed to living one's life from the perspective that life is everlasting. Since religions generally contain an eternal perspective within their worldviews, secularism is demonstrated in actions that seek to restrict religious views or considerations from influencing public policies and activities.

13 The notion that conceptions of truth and morality are not absolute but relative to the individuals or groups holding them. It holds that all criteria of judgment in particular situations are relative for the individuals involved apart from any fixed standards.

14 James Swindal, "Faith and Reason", Internet Encyclopedia Of Philosophy, par. 1 (2001 [cited 1 May 2002]) ; available from the World Wide Web at http://www.utm.edu/research/iep/f/faith-re.htm.

15 Danish philosopher Soren Kierkegaard argued that one's religious faith is a "leap" in the sense that it does not rest upon anything rational

to support it.

16 TORCASO v. WATKINS, 367 U.S. 488 (1961).

17 UNITED STATES v. SEEGER, 380 U.S. 163 (1965).

18 John W. Whitehead, *The Second American Revolution* (Westchester, IL: Crossway Books, 1982), p. 108.

19 Paul Copan, *Is Everything Really Relative?* (Norcross, GA: Ravi Zacharias International Ministries, 1999), p.p. 24-26.

20 Greg Bahnsen, "Apologetics in Practice," *The Covenant Herald* (Newport, DE: Basileians Newsletter, 1991), p. 1.

21 Kenneth Gentry, "In Defense of Creedalism," *Penpoint*, (Southern California Center for Christian Studies, Volume 9, Number 4, December 1998), p. 1.

22 Kenneth Gentry, "In Defense of Creedalism," *Penpoint*, (Southern California Center for Christian Studies, Volume 9, Number 4, December 1998), p. 1.

23 D. James Kennedy, *Knowing The Whole Truth* (Old Tappan, NJ: Fleming H. Revell Company, 1985), p. 17.

24 An excellent summary of biblical Christian theology is contained in the "Westminster Confession of Faith".

25 Henry C. Theissen, *Lectures in Systematic Theology* (Grand Rapids, MI: William B. Erdmans, 1949), p. 89.

26 Henry C. Theissen, *Lectures in Systematic Theology* (Grand Rapids, MI: William B. Erdmans, 1949), p. 89.

27 Cornelius Van Til, *A Defense Of The Faith* (Phillipsburg, NJ: Presbyterian and Reformed, 1955), p. 9.

28 Cornelius Van Til, *A Defense Of The Faith* (Phillipsburg, NJ: Presbyterian and Reformed, 1955), p. 9.

29 Cornelius Van Til, *A Defense Of The Faith* (Phillipsburg, NJ: Presbyterian and Reformed, 1955), p. 10.

30 Louis Berkhoff, *Summary of Christian Doctrine* (Grand Rapids, MI: WM. B. EERDMANS, 1938), p.59-60.

31 Cornelius Van Til quoted in Greg Bahnsen, *Van Til's Apologetic-Readings and Analysis* (Phillipsburg, NJ: Presbyterian & Reformed Publishing, 1998), p. 224.

32 Richard L. Pratt Jr., *Every Thought Captive* (Phillipsburg, NJ: Presbyterian and Reformed Publishing Co., 1979), p. 29.

33 Louis Berkhoff, *Summary of Christian Doctrine* (Grand Rapids, MI: WM. B. EERDMANS, 1938), p. 76.

34 John Blanchard, *Ultimate Questions* (Durham, Eng.: Evangelical Press, 1987), p. 21.

35 "Westminster Confession of Faith", Chapter 8, Section 5.

36 John McRay quoted in Lee Strobel, *The Case For Christ* (Grand Rapids, MI: Zondervan Publishing House, 1998), p. 100.

37 Thomas Thompson, "Face To Face: Biblical Minimalists Meet Their

Challengers," *Biblical Archeology Review*, (July/August 1997, Vol 23 No. 4), p. 28.

38 Louis Berkhof, *Principles of Biblical Interpretation* (Grand Rapids, MI: Baker Book House, 1950), p. 40. (Hermeneutics is the study of methods for interpretation.)

39 Gary North, *The Hoax Of Higher Criticism* (Tyler, TX: Institute for Christian Economics, 1989), p. 3.

40 George Ladd quoted in J. Barton Payne, "Higher Criticism And Biblical Inerrancy," *Inerrancy*, Norman L. Geisler ed., (Grand Rapids, MI: Zondervan Publishing House, 1980), p. 90.

41 Walter C. Kaiser Jr., "Legitimate Hermeneutics," *Inerrancy*, Norman L. Geisler ed. (Grand Rapids, MI: Zondervan Publishing House, 1980), p. 138.

42 Robert R. Booth, "Of Taste Buds: Calvin's Apologetic," *Penpoint* (Placentia, CA: Southern California Center For Christian Studies, Vol. 7, No, 10, Nov. 1996), p.3.

43 J. Barton Payne, "Higher Criticism And Biblical Inerrancy," *Inerrancy*, Norman L. Geisler ed., (Grand Rapids, MI: Zondervan Publishing House, 1980), p. 96.

44 A. H. Strong quoted in P.C. Nelson, *Bible Doctrines* (Springfield, Missouri: Gospel Publishing House, 1948), p. 6.

45 J. Barton Payne, "Higher Criticism And Biblical Inerrancy" *Inerrancy*, Norman L. Geisler ed., (Grand Rapids, MI: Zondervan Publishing House, 1980), p. 93.

46 Gary North, *The Hoax Of Higher Criticism* (Tyler, TX: Institute for Christian Economics, 1989), pp. 30-31.

47 Rudolf Bultman quoted in Earle E. Cairns, *Christianity Through The Centuries* (Grand Rapids, MI: Academie Books, 1954), p. 446.

48 Gary North, *The Hoax Of Higher Criticism* (Tyler, TX: Institute for Christian Economics, 1989), p. 3.

49 A. Momigliano quoted in Craig L. Bloomberg, "The Legitimacy And Limits Of Harmonization", *Hermeneutics, Authority, And Canon*, D.A. Carson and John D. Woodbridge ed., (Grand Rapids, MI: Baker Books, 1985), p. 173.

50 Gleason L. Archer, "Alleged Errors And Discrepancies In The Original Manuscripts Of The Bible", *Inerrancy*, Norman L. Geisler ed. (Grand Rapids, MI: Zondervan Publishing House, 1980), p. 58.

51 Ian Murray, Evangelicalism Divided (Carlisle, PA: The Banner Of Truth Trust, 2000), p. 20.

52 Cornelius Van Til, *The Defense Of The Faith* (Phillipsburg, NJ: Presbyterian & Reformed Publishing, 1955), p. 8.

53 Literally meaning "from that which is before".

54 Dan McCartney and Charles Clayton, *Let The Reader Understand* (Wheaton, Ill: Victor Books, 1994), p. 15.

Endnotes

55 J.I. Packer and Thomas Howard, "Meet Secular Humanism," in *Salt and Light*, ed. David J. Gyertson (Dallas, TX: Word Publishing, 1993), p. 70.

56 Cornelius Van Til quoted in Greg Bahnsen, "Van Til's Call For A Distinctive Christian Mindset," *Penpoint* (Southern California Center For Christian Studies, Vol. 6, No.4, April 1995), p. 2.

57 Francis A. Schaeffer, *Trilogy* (Westchester, Illinois: Crossway Books, 1990), p. 266.

58 Francis A. Schaeffer, *Trilogy* (Westchester, Illinois: Crossway Books, 1990), p. 185.

59 Dan McCartney and Charles Clayton, *Let The Reader Understand* (Wheaton, Ill: Victor Books, 1994), p. 22.

60 Dan McCartney and Charles Clayton, *Let The Reader Understand* (Wheaton, Ill: Victor Books, 1994), pp. 15-16.

61 Tim LaHaye, *The Battle for the Mind* (Old Tappan, NJ: Fleming H. Revell Co., 1980), p. 49.

62 Richard L. Pratt, Jr. *Every Thought Captive* (Phillipsburg, NJ: Presbyterian & Reformed Publishing Co., 1979), p. 17.

63 Greg Bahnsen, *Always Ready* (Texarkana, AR: Covenant Media Foundation, 1996), pp. 4-5.

64 Dan McCartney and Charles Clayton, *Let The Reader Understand* (Wheaton, Ill: Victor Books, 1994), p. 14.

65 Greg Bahnsen, *Always Ready* (Texarkana, AR: Covenant Media Foundation, 1996), p. 123.

66 Greg Bahnsen, *Always Ready* (Texarkana, AR: Covenant Media Foundation, 1996), p. 72.

67 Dan McCartney and Charles Clayton, *Let The Reader Understand* (Wheaton, Ill: Victor Books, 1994), p. 26.

68 Cornelius Van Til, *The Defense Of The Faith* (Phillipsburg, NJ: Presbyterian and Reformed Publishing Co., 1955), p. 298.

69 Aldous Huxley, *Ends and Means* (London: Chatto & Windus, 1946), p. 273.

70 Michael Butler, "A Truly reformed Epistemology," *Penpoint*, (Placentia, CA: Southern California Center For Christian Studies, Vol. 8, No. 5, May 1997), p.3.

71 Richard L. Pratt Jr., *Every Thought Captive* (Phillipsburg, NJ: Presbyterian and Reformed Publishing Co., 1979), p. 94.

72 Greg Bahnsen, *Always Ready* (Texarkana, AR: Covenant Media Foundation, 1996), p. 75.

73 David Hume, "The Argument From Evil," *Readings In The Philosophy Of Religion* (Englewood Cliffs, NJ: Prentice-Hall, Inc., Baruch A. Brody, ed., 1974), p. 270.

74 C.S. Lewis, *The Problem Of Pain* (New York: Macmillan Publishing Co., 1962), p. 26.

75 Ravi Zacharias, *A Shattered Visage – The Real Face Of Atheism* (Grand Rapids, MI: Baker Books, 1990), p. 139.

76 Kenneth D. Boa, "What Is Behind Morality," *Living Ethically In The 90's* (Wheaton, Ill: SP Publications, J. Kerby Anderson, ed., 1990), p. 40.

77 Ravi Zacharias, *Can Man Live Without God* (Dallas, TX: Word Publishing, 1994), p. 14.

78 Bob Slosser, *Changing the Way America Thinks* (Dallas, TX: Word Publishing, 1989), p. 148.

79 Cornelius Van Til quoted in Greg Bahnsen, *Van Til's Apologetic* (Phillipsburg, NJ: Presbyterian & Reformed, 1998), p. 190.

80 Gleason L. Archer, *Encyclopedia of Bible Difficulties* (Grand Rapids, MI: Zondervan Publishing House, 1982), pp. 55-56.

81 Michael Butler, "The Great Debate Gets Personal," *Penpoint* (Placentia, CA: Southern California Center For Christian Studies, Vol. 7 No. 7, 1996), p. 3.

82 Kenneth D. Boa, "What Is Behind Morality," *Living Ethically In The 90's* (Wheaton, Ill: SP Publications, J. Kerby Anderson, ed., 1990), p. 39.

83 Kenneth D. Boa, "What Is Behind Morality," *Living Ethically In The 90's* (Wheaton, Ill: SP Publications, J. Kerby Anderson, ed., 1990), p. 39.

84 Ingrid Newkirk quoted in Fred Barnes, "Politics," *Vogue*, September 1989, p. 542. Ingrid Newkirk is co-founder of People for the Ethical Treatment of Animals (PeTA).

85 Ravi Zacharias, *A Shattered Visage* (Grand Rapids, MI: Baker Books, 1990), pp. 77,78,79.

86 Douglas Wilson, "Disputatio – Justifying Non-Christian Objections", in Wilson-Till Debate par. 11 [cited 1 May 2002] ; available from the World Wide Web at http://www.reformed.org/apologetics/credenda-agenda/wilsontill. html. This exchange between Christian Pastor Douglas Wilson and professing atheist Farrell Till originally appeared in the online e-zine Credenda/Agenda (Vol. 7; No. 1).

87 *Nihilism* refers to the doctrine of meaninglessness.

88 Greg Bahnsen, *Van Til's Apologetic* (Phillipsburg, NJ: Presbyterian & Reformed, 1998), p. 235.

89 Cornelius Van Til quoted in Greg Bahnsen, *Van Til's Apologetic* (Phillipsburg, NJ: Presbyterian & Reformed, 1998), p. 237.

90 Greg Bahnsen, *Van Til's Apologetic* (Phillipsburg, NJ: Presbyterian & Reformed, 1998), p. 239.

91 Cornelius Van Til quoted in Greg Bahnsen, *Van Til's Apologetic* (Phillipsburg, NJ: Presbyterian & Reformed, 1998), p. 190.

92 George Gaylord Simpson, quoted in Philip Johnson, *Darwin On*

Trial (Downer's Grove, Ill.: InterVarsity Press, 1991), p. 116.

93 Francis A. Schaeffer, *No Final Conflict* (Downers Grove, Ill.: InterVarsity Press, 1975), p. 18.

94 Stephen Jay Gould, "Dorothy, It's Really Oz," *Time*, (August 23, 1999), p. 59.

95 Philip Johnson, *Darwin On Trial* (Downer's Grove, Ill.: InterVarsity Press, 1991), p. 8-9.

96 Charles Colson, *A Dance With Deception* (Dallas, TX: Word Publishing, 1993), p. 222.

97 Neal Gillespie, *Charles Darwin and the Problem of Creation* (Chicago: University of Chicago Press, 1979), p. 19.

98 Nancy R. Percey and Charles B. Thaxton, *The Soul Of Science* (Wheaton, Ill: Crossway Books, 1994), p. 246.

99 Greg Bahnsen, *Always Ready* (Texarkana, AR: Covenant Media Foundation, 1996), p. 230.

100 Deism teaches that God created the cosmos and then backed off, allowing it to operate on its own through impersonal natural laws.

101 Greg Bahnsen, *Always Ready* (Texarkana, AR: Covenant Media Foundation, 1996), p. 229.

102 Greg Bahnsen, *Always Ready* (Texarkana, AR: Covenant Media Foundation, 1996), p. 121.

103 Carl Hermann Voss, *In Search Of Meaning-Living Religions of the World* (Cleveland, OH: World Publishing Co., 1968), p. 44.

104 Ramakrishna quoted in Huston Smith, *The World's Religions* (New York: HarperCollins, 1958), p. 74.

105 Huston Smith, *The World's Religions* (New York: HarperCollins Publishers, 1958), p. 13.

106 Ravi Zacharias, *Jesus Among Other Gods* (Nashville, TN: Word Publishing, 2000), p. 7.

107 Ravi Zacharias, *Jesus Among Other Gods* (Nashville, TN: Word Publishing, 2000), p. 55.

108 Huston Smith, *The World's Religions* (New York: HarperCollins Publishers, 1958), p. 60.

109 Huston Smith, *The World's Religions* (New York: HarperCollins Publishers, 1958), p. 62.

110 Andree Seu, "Divine Visitation," *World Magazine* (Nov. 18, 2000), p. 28.

111 Huston Smith, *The World's Religions* (New York: HarperCollins Publishers, 1958), p. 64.

112 Robert Hume, *The World's Living Religions* (New York: Charles Scribner's Sons, 1924), p. 32.

113 *Great Religions of the World* (Washington, DC: National Geographic Society, 1971), p. 39.

114 Chandogya Upanishad, 5.10.7.

115 TPU 289, Sacred Books of the East 15:63, quoted in Robert Hume, *The World's Living Religions* (New York: Charles Scribner's Sons, 1924), p. 27.

116 Robert Hume, *The World's Living Religions* (New York: Charles Scribner's Sons, 1924), p.32.

117 Carl Hermann Voss, *In Search Of Meaning* (Cleveland, OH: World Pub. Co., 1968), p. 40.

118 Quoted in Huston Smith, *The World's Religions* (New York: HarperCollins Publishers, 1958), p. 74.

119 Carl Hermann Voss, *In Search Of Meaning* (Cleveland, OH: World Pub. Co., 1968), p. 42.

120 Ravi Zacharias, *Jesus Among Other Gods* (Nashville, TN: Word Publishing, 2000), p. 97.

121 R.J. Rushdoony, "The Sovereignty of God," *Chalcedon Report* (Vallecito, CA: July 2000, No.420), p. 2.

122 Paul K. Moser, *Why Isn't God More Obvious?* (Norcross, GA: Ravi Zacharias International Ministries, 2000), p. 18.

123 Paul K. Moser, *Why Isn't God More Obvious?* (Norcross, GA: Ravi Zacharias International Ministries, 2000), p. 33.

124 C.S. Lewis, *Mere Christianity* (New York: Macmillan Publishing Co., 1943), p. 136.

125 Richard L. Pratt, Jr., *Every Thought Captive* (Phillipsburg, NJ: Presbyterian & Reformed Publishing Co., 1979), p. 29.

126 Robert R. Booth, "Of Taste Buds: Calvin's Apologetic," *Penpoint* (Placentia, CA: Southern California Center for Christian Studies, Vol. 7, No. 10, 1996), pp. 1-2.

127 Greg Bahnsen, *Van Til's Apologetic* (Phillipsburg, NJ: Presbyterian & Reformed Publishing, 1998), pp. 111-112.